N31395

Interpreting the
Medical Literature

Interpreting the Medical Literature

A Clinician's Guide

Stephen H. Gehlbach, M.D., M.P.H.
Associate Professor
Department of Community and Family
* Medicine*
Duke University Medical Center
Durham, North Carolina

MACMILLAN PUBLISHING COMPANY
NEW YORK

Collier Macmillan Canada, Inc.
TORONTO

Collier Macmillan Publishers
LONDON

Macmillan Publishing Company
866 Third Avenue, New York, New York 10022

Collier Macmillan Canada, Inc.

Collier Macmillan Publishers - London

International Standard Book Number: 0-02-341260-7

Library of Congress Catalog Card Number: 81-65128

Printing: 2 3 4 5 6 7 8   Year: 5 6 7 8 9 0 1 2 3

Contents

Preface

The purpose of this book is to provide clinicians with an approach to reading and understanding research articles that appear in medical journals. Although it is not a text of epidemiology, it is based on principles of that discipline and on a way of thinking that is epidemiological. The terms used in discussing concepts will come primarily from epidemiology rather than from the social sciences research tradition. Most medical readers will already have some familiarity with jargon, such as "case-control and cohort studies," "sensitivity and specificity," and "relative risk." Understanding these terms is essential to comprehending medical articles, / and they will be discussed in modest detail; but because the book is intended as a guide for clinicians—people who need to make practical use of medical literature—extensive forays into epidemiology's semantic jungle will be avoided. Some depth will be sacrificed for the sake of brevity. The goal is to acquire skill with a few fundamental analytical tools and avoid becoming mired in complexity.

Like all medical books, this one will suffer from opinion. It is one person's approach to understanding medical literature and is subject to personal preference, slanted interpretation, contrariness, and the other ills that publishing opinion is heir to. In self-defense, it should be noted that this approach to interpreting the literature has been used on family-medicine residents for the past five years and has met with reasonable success. There is, in fact, written documentation providing meager evidence that doctors can learn and successfully apply principles of critical reading [1]. After finishing this book, readers may wish to try on their skills by criticizing an article that claims that critical reading skills can be successfully taught.

The book is intended for several levels of clinical learners. It is hoped that medical students, who are beginning to form reading habits, will benefit from an early exposure to the concepts of ade-

ix

quate study design, appropriate sample selection, and use of statistical inference. More seasoned clinicians should become more comfortable with old stumbling blocks, such as "selection bias" and "the null hypothesis." Because clinical applicability and relevance are major goals, I have elected to use illustrations that come from published articles. The sparkle of authenticity that this provides is somewhat tarnished by the appearance of being critical toward colleagues. None of the critiques of examples used in this book is intended to be disparaging of the authors. Conducting good clinical research is a formidable task. There is substantial risk in exposing one's work to the harsh light of publication. Because of the difficulties inherent in studying and documenting the behavior of humans, it is a rare study indeed that is beyond fault. I think the advantages of using published articles exceed the liabilities. Real examples give readers the opportunity to examine primary sources for themselves, practice their analytical skills, and formulate dissenting views.

A final admonition. As with developing clinical skills, such as examining tympanic membranes or listening for heart murmurs, acquiring proficiency in reading the medical literature requires practice. Most of the principles discussed in this book will appear simple and are reasonably straightforward—but that is not to say that their application will come easily to everyone. Facility and comfort will come only through practice. Like visualizing the fundus of the eye, it is not difficult once you get the hang of it, but it takes work to develop and maintain the skill.

Acknowledgments

Many colleagues in Duke's Community and Family Medicine Department supplied advice and good cheer. Marcie gave tireless support. Hilary, Hunter, and Carol were very patient.

Reference

1. Gehlbach, S. H., Bobula, J. A., and Dickinson, J. C. Teaching residents to read the medical literature. *J. Med. Educ.* 55:362–365, 1980.

Interpreting the Medical Literature

ONE

Tasting an Article

*Some books are to be tasted, others to be swallowed, and
some few to be chewed and digested.*
—Francis Bacon

Keeping up with the medical literature is a strenuous
proposition. The stacks of unread journals that collect on desks and
in filing cabinets during medical school and residency training only
grow larger. The number of textbooks, yearbooks, newsletters, and
specialty journals swells while the time to read them shrinks. Yet we
are pressed to keep current from several sides. Most of us are taught
early in medical training that to be a good physician one must keep
abreast of the latest in clinical syndromes, novel diagnostic tests, and
innovative treatments. We need to learn which environmental car-
cinogens to avoid and how to improve our understanding of the
causes of heart disease. Specialty boards and medical societies rein-
force this concept by requiring documentation of continuing education for certification and for society membership. Some recertification
plans specifically call for examinations based on information from the
current literature.

Patients also expect informed physicians. Like their doctors,
they are beset with medical facts and fiction from radio, television,
and the popular press. Whether they read the *New York Times* or a
supermarket tabloid, they are likely to be getting information that is at
least in part based on reports from the medical literature. Patients
want to know about their risk of contracting Legionnaire's disease
when they visit Philadelphia, whether their headaches deserve a
CAT scan, or if Dr. Nocals' water-only diet really works.

Even though the spirit may be willing, the eyes grow weak, and

1

the task of sorting through the mounds of published material seems a losing affair. Some remedy would appear to come from the many secondary sources that are available. Medical textbooks, special review journals, newsletters, and audio cassettes supply synthesized information on current topics. One can easily read the collected opinions of experts about everything from ankylosing spondylitis to tropical zoonoses from one of several excellent textbooks, or listen to a learned colleague discuss lead poisoning while driving to work, thanks to the wonders of magnetic tape. Secondary sources are an efficient way to gather information and circumvent the painful process of trying to master the complicated presentation of data in primary sources. Experts have problems like the rest of us. Sometimes their subjective selves get the upper hand and cast controversy into fact. Opinions and biased reading can become standard knowledge. That should not surprise us since many studies are open to differing interpretation. It does mean, however, that while texts and reviews are useful, none of us can depend entirely on secondary sources for our information. We need to be able to evaluate a primary research article ourselves and judge its value.

Finding time to do this reading is not the only challenge. Articles describing clinical studies have become increasingly sophisticated. Not only has the complexity of the information presented increased, the methods used to obtain and interpret data have become correspondingly complex. Clinical studies now utilize "stratified sampling techniques," "randomized-double-blind-crossover designs," and a multitude of semicomprehensible techniques for statistical analysis. Understanding the nuances of these methodologies is every bit as demanding as keeping up with the side effects of the latest pharmacological agents or the newest discoveries of immune-cell function.

The purpose of this book is to give practical aid to the beleaguered clinician. This chapter will offer advice on general approaches to reading articles—on exercising our powers of selectivity and efficiency. As Francis Bacon suggested some 300 years ago, much of the written material that comes our way deserves only a perfunctory taste with relatively few articles meriting full digestion.

Once we have developed some rules for making initial decisions about which articles to read and have gained an overall sense of what they are about, we can proceed with more detailed critical review. Chapters will be devoted to exploring the design of studies, classifying methodologies and learning about their basic strengths and weaknesses. The problems encountered in making measurements and collecting data in a satisfactory manner will be a second concern; we will examine observer and subject biases. Finally, ways in which data are analyzed and interpreted will be discussed.

The goal of all this will be to arrive at an interpretation we can call our own. We will balance the strengths and flaws uncovered in an article and come up with an independent assessment of whether the author's message rings true—whether in the final analysis acupuncture successfully reduces pain or treating mild hypertension lowers morbidity from stroke. The bottom line is validity. Are the results believable? Do they represent the truth? Are they applicable to our practice? Will the patients we see and treat respond in the same way as those described in the study? Does the paper really support its claims?

Validity

The concept of validity is central to the critical analysis of the medical literature. We will continue to encounter it in several forms throughout the book. Two types of validity will be of concern. The first relates to the internal structure of the study. In their discussion of experimental designs, Campbell and Stanley call it internal validity [6]. They mean that within the confines of the study results appear to be accurate, the methods and analysis used bear up under scrutiny, and the interpretation of the investigators appears supported. For the particular subjects evaluated, hydrochlorothiazide appears to be better than placebo in reducing high blood pressure, smokers seem to experience more chronic lung disease than nonsmokers, or obstetrical units with fetal-monitoring devices have lower rates of perinatal problems. Truth is told.

There is another type of validity that we will discuss. Called external validity by the social scientists [6], it is more commonly thought of by medical people as generalizability. Generalizability is terribly important to clinicians. It has to do with whether conclusions (if internally valid) can be applied to the reader's setting or practice. We will return to it in later chapters.

Reasons to Read

I have already alluded to the general goal of keeping current as a reason for reading journals. Medical journals offer more than reports of recent information on tests, treatments, and concepts of etiology. They provide a fascinating potpourri of opinion, philosophy, argument, gossip, history, theory, and advice. I have mentioned the topical review articles that condense up-to-date thoughts on the treatment of congestive heart failure or use of ultrasound technology. Individual authors may be responsible for these reports or, occasionally, expert committees publish their consensus on a controversial topic, such as, the treatment of febrile seizures or the prophylactic use of antibiotics in hospitals. Practical hints, such as diagnosing scabies in the office or setting up pension plans for employees, are features of some journals. Comments published as letters to the journal and sage remarks made by the editors can make engaging and informative reading. These are especially valuable when they offer informed critiques of research articles or when authors debate the results of research in an open forum. There are pieces that discuss aspects of the history of the profession (a review of small-pox immunization in early Boston), views from other parts of the medical world, or philosophical pieces on the wonders and frailties of our medical system.

That is a splendid array of offerings, and I have not mentioned the book reviews, employment opportunities, and news of professional organizations. Any of this list makes legitimate reading, but none falls into the category of primary research, which is the meat for our discussion. Among the new ideas and information available to readers are the choices listed in table 1–1. They span a spectrum from learning about new diseases like toxic-shock syndrome or Legionnaire's disease to sharing the collective experience of colleagues who used antimicrobials during the last thirty years in the Boston City Hospital.

This rich smorgasbord is worth noting since reasons for picking up a journal will vary. The approach one takes in reading an article depends very much on the intent at the outset. Reading to review the pathophysiology of Rocky Mountain spotted fever or to learn what an expert committee thinks is the proper way to work up a urinary-tract infection is a different process from assessing the validity of a report linking artificial sweeteners to bladder cancer or the results of a

Table 1-1 Some Reasons for Reading Medical Articles

Read to Find Out About:	*For Example:*
New Diseases	Toxic-shock syndrome [8]
	Legionnaire's disease [14]
New Presentations or Manifestations of Known Disease	An outbreak of foodborne giardiasis [19]
	Rickets developing in children on fad diets [9]
Natural History of Diseases	The natural history of bacteriuria in schoolgirls [10]
	The function of patients with unexplained chest pain 16 months after normal angiography [18]
New Diagnostic Procedures	Use of Gram stain to diagnose streptococcal throat [7]
	Outcomes of fetal monitoring [20]
New Treatments or Programs	Use of ice bags to stop tachycardias [5]
	Cimetidine to prevent gastrointestinal bleeding [21]
	Patient satisfaction with a new continuity clinic [4]
Side Effects	Hepatitis in patients receiving INH [15]
	Increased absenteeism among newly diagnosed hypertensives [11]
Causes (and Noncauses) and Predictors of Disease	Artificial sweeteners and bladder cancer [13]
	Type of medical school and resident performance [17]
What's Gone On Before/The Experience of Others	Use of antimicrobials in general hospitals [12]
	The ecology of dog bites in St. Louis [3]

study demonstrating the benefits of a new antacid for treating peptic ulcers. Deciding in advance what you wish to obtain from the journal is the first step to more efficient reading.

Understanding the framework of articles also facilitates efficient reading. Mortimer Adler has produced an entire volume on how to read a book [1]. In it he emphasizes that effective reading requires identifying and understanding the structure or components of a work. That, he states, contributes to the "intelligibility of the whole." Adler's advise on reading books has parallels for the reader of medical journals. His medical metaphor to approaching a great book has an irresistible message for clinicians:

> Every book has a skeleton hidden between its boards. Your job is to find it. A book comes to you with flesh on its bare bones and clothes over its flesh. It is all dressed up. I am not asking you to be impolite or cruel. You do not have to undress it or tear the flesh off its limbs to get at the firm structure that underlies the soft. But you must read the book with x-ray eyes, for it is an essential part of your first apprehension of any book to grasp its structure [1].

The Bones of an Article

Most articles that deliver new information to readers share a basic structural plan. The six main sections outlined in table 1–2 are usually present.

The *summary or abstract* should present a concise statement of the goal or hypothesis of the study, a word or two about how the endeavor was undertaken, highlights of the results, and a concluding thought that puts it all into perspective. Summaries used to be placed at the end of articles, but in recent years have come to occupy a prominent place at the beginning, standing out in boldface or italic to provide busy readers with a quick, efficient way of sampling the journal. One should be able to glean a reasonable sense of the contents of a journal by flipping past the laxative and antacid advertisements and reading just the abstracts. One could do worse than be a reader of abstracts. One sometimes needs to do better, however. Abstracts provide a useful taste of the contents of the study, but they are rarely sufficient to make a meal in themselves. Because of the

Table 1-2 The Basic Structure of an Article

Section:	Look for:
Abstract/Summary	Overview or summary of the work
	Highlights of results
	General statement of significance
Introduction	Background information: history, pathophysiology, clinical presentation
	Review of the work of others
	Rationale for present study
Methods/Materials & Methods/Patients & Methods	Study design
	Subject-selection procedures
	Methods of measurement
	Description of analytic techniques
Results	What happened?
	Graphics—tables, charts, figures—that summarize findings
Discussion/Comment/Conclusion	Meaning, significance of work
	Critique of study: discussion of limitations as well as strengths, further analysis
	Comparison with work of others
	Disclaimers, equivocation, apologies, chest thumping, speculation, instruction, fantasy, and so on
References/Bibliography	Evidence that work of others has been considered
	Leads to further exploration of the subject

need to be concise, abstracts select only the highlights of a paper. They are also, quite understandably, an author's attempt to put his best foot forward. Sometimes the author's summary of the article contains more wish than reality and presents a distorted view of the work that follows. Deception is probably not intended, but vigorous condensation has imparted an unfaithful flavor.

An example is a paper that takes up the challenging problem of diagnosing the cause of fever in young children [16]. In an innovative approach, the investigators take a standard inpatient diagnostic tool, the blood culture, and apply it to patients in a pediatric walk-in clinic. Success is announced as the abstract states that, "The data suggest that in this setting, a blood culture provides valuable help in establishing the specific bacteriologic diagnosis in febrile children without focal signs of infection." Now that's great news! Anyone who has cared for young children has spent more than one restless night ruminating over the 18-month-old toddler who was sent home from the clinic with a temperature of 40°C and for whom no source of infection could be found after a diligent physical examination. These children who are "without focal signs of infection" present a dilemma for the clinician. Any diagnostic help is willingly accepted! But does this paper provide the salvation that the abstract claims? The article does document the incidence of positive blood cultures among a number of these young patients, describes the organisms responsible for the bacteremia, and provides some evidence that the phenomenon of the positive blood culture occurs more frequently among younger children who have very high fevers. What it does not do is demonstrate that these children were without focal signs of infection. A careful reading reveals that, in fact, 14 percent of the total population studied had chest roentgenograms that showed pulmonary infiltrates. Now that certainly suggests a focus of infection. Ten of the 31 patients who eventually had pathogenic bacteria isolated from their blood had radiologic evidence of pneumonia—a pretty reasonable source for their fevers. What is more, the paper does not mention any clinical features of the illnesses nor what criteria were used in the evaluation to exclude focal signs. We do not know if everyone got their ears examined for possible otitis media or who had a rash suggestive of scarlet fever. We are left with little confidence that the group of children described in the paper are as the abstract advertises. Abstracts can be read to gain a sense of a paper's content but cannot supply sufficient information to judge validity.

The *introduction* section of the paper usually provides background information on the topic to be addressed, as well as rationale for why the authors undertook the adventure. Sometimes the introduction will offer an extended review of other literature surrounding the topic. When well done, this provides readers with a nourishing appetizer before they undertake the main course of the paper and may in itself make the reading worthwhile.

The next section describes the *methodology* of the study. It is labelled "Materials and Methods," "Patients and Methods," or other variations on that theme. It details the patient populations studied, study designs utilized, and data-collection techniques employed, and it describes in more detail than many of us care to know the analytical and evaluative procedures used in the course of the study. This is the section that most readers skip. In fact, it is the section that many journals relegate to small print. It is also the section to which we will devote much of our analytical energy and to which we will return repeatedly in future chapters.

The *results* section, quite logically, presents the information obtained from the execution of the study. Results are usually found both in the text and in accompanying tables, charts, graphs, and figures. Analysis and some interpretation of the data are also presented in the results section. Like the methods section, the results section represents an essential part of the main bill of fare and will be discussed at considerable length.

An interesting mix of ingredients can go into fashioning the *discussion* of an article. A further analysis of the results may be accomplished; results and conclusions of other studies may be compared and contrasted; the author may offer apologies for oversights and transgressions or build a case to strengthen and support results. The discussion section is usually the most speculative and often the most interesting reading in the medical paper. Authors may review and comment upon other studies related to their own and usually try to place the results in perspective. It can make especially entertaining reading if the author's interpretation of the work is different from your own.

A list of *references* or bibliography usually finishes off an article. Little more need be said about the references except that they are most conspicuous in their absence. Few authors are writing on topics so novel that some thought and other research has not gone on before. The list of references gives a reader a clue to how diligently authors have researched and reviewed the experience of other workers. An extensive, well-done bibliography that provides easy access to a wide selection of articles on a topic can save hours of hunting through library reference works and is sometimes the saving grace of an otherwise lackluster journal article.

Having a firm idea of what you wish to gain from reading a journal and knowing how to utilize the framework of an article to best advantage gets you off to a proper start. With this background, a few rules for sampling the literature are needed.

Approaching an Article

Read Only What Is Interesting and Useful

Whether the cause is overzealous toilet training or the result of an oppressive system of early education, most of us have acquired a disquieting degree of compulsive behavior by the time we reach medical school or clinical practice. This trait is not without value. It helps us master the many facts that form the foundation of our clinical practice and drives us to persist in attacking a patient's ketoacidosis at two o'clock in the morning. However, compulsiveness has its liabilities as well. Confronted with a burgeoning pile of medical journals, we cannot bear the thought that any of the information packaged within the glossy pages should go unlearned. We wait for that magical time when we can sit down and plow through it. That day never arrives, and our guilt grows proportionally with the stack, diminishing only occasionally when a few spare hours prunes the pile by one or two or when a housekeeping purge assigns it all irrevocably to the attic or trash bin. Mental health demands that we become more selective readers. Rather than trying to devour every article encountered, we need to develop tactics for sampling journals and consuming only those articles that are most nutritious.

Our first taste of an article should have a selective purpose. What is the article about? Is it a topic of interest? Is the information likely to be useful? If an article is not of interest, do not read it! There is plenty of information overloading our synapses as it is. There is no point in burdening the system with information that will not be used. It takes up time and space and probably will not be retained. Of course there is a risk in making choices. The case report dismissed as unworthy after a quick look may well be just like a case that strolls into your office next Friday or becomes the topic of a discussion at grand rounds. So be it. Selective reading is an even greater problem for students, who must feed omnivorously to define their areas of interest and for whom examinations and interrogating attending physicians are everpresent incentives to acquire information. It is probably at this stage in the development of a medical career that bad reading habits develop and the sense of duty to read indiscriminately becomes entrenched. The solution to the problem is simple in concept and difficult in execution.

1. Scan the table of contents and decide what each article is about.

2. Select articles to be pursued in greater detail and bypass those that are not of interest. (The faint of heart who are reluctant to make this decision on the basis of a title alone may consult the abstract.)

3. Do not equivocate. Do not accumulate a pile of maybes. Articles that might be useful in the future but are of little interest now usually do not get read. All of us like to hedge our bets against that time when we will encounter that rare new genetic syndrome or want to know how to treat a patient with glycogen storage disease, but medical libraries are full of just such advice. Pursue such information when the special need arises.

Scan the Article to Gain a Quick Overview

An important corollary to selective reading is to hold back the initial impulse to bite right into an article. Step back for a brief, circumspect view of the whole. You may be surprised at what you discover. Finding page after page of uninterrupted, double-column print may permanently dampen your enthusiasm or relegate the piece to a day when you really do have more time to spend. A quick flip through may tell you that the technical complexity of the article is more than you are prepared to take on. Unintelligible jargon or complicated mathematical formulas may suggest your reading time would be more profitably spent elsewhere. You may discover on this quick perusal that an article you thought would offer practical clinical tidbits is actually the report of highly specialized laboratory work—a piece listed in the contents as "Cow's Milk Allergy" turns out to report on "the production of a lymphokine, the leukocyte-migration-inhibition factor, by peripheral blood lymphocytes in response to an in vitro challenge with bovine beta-lactoglobulin" [2]—or that an article in which you anticipated exciting new information is only a revival of some well-known old facts. Look over the graphs and tables. These are particularly useful in giving a perspective since they are usually carefully selected by authors to summarize the main messages of the piece (worth more than many thousand words, as they say).

Scanning gives the reader a sense of the structure of an article, a perspective in which to organize thoughts. Many articles will, within the basic framework already described, offer subheadings that facilitate this structuring process. Scan them. A competent author, as Adler suggests, has organized the architecture of a work to be a functional, intelligible guide to the whole.

Concentrate on the Methods Section

Once one decides that an article is worth reading and one's appetite has not been dulled by the quick scan, a new approach is needed. Most readers begin and end with the abstract. We have already seen the dangers in relying on that overly condensed bit of information. Those with the fortitude to take on more of the article generally proceed to the introduction, pale at the prospect of reading the small print in the methods section and skip it. Sometimes they also pass over tedious presentations of results in favor of finding out what happens at the end. Since the author usually rehashes the results and offers an overall interpretation of the study in the discussion section, heading straight for the last section seems an economical way to proceed. One purpose of this book is to retrain clinicians to focus on the methodology. Read the methods section first. Here is the substance of the research. Any new information, no matter how enthusiastically discussed or fervently endorsed, is only as useful as the methods and results are sound. Once we train ourselves to look critically at articles, the discussion sections in many will become superfluous. The design or analysis in an article may be so deficient that no amount of explanation, extrapolation, or apology on the part of the author can set it right. In this case, we have saved reading time by not pursuing the discussion of a study that is so marred that any conclusions made would lack validity.

Reserve the Right of Final Judgment

One last and very important principle remains. The ultimate interpretation and decision about the value of an article rests with the reader. Too frequently clinicians are cowed by the power of the printed word. After all, the author has reviewed the literature, designed and executed the study, and presented a convincing array of results. Who are we to quibble with the interpretation? It is only reasonable to defer to the experts. That is why reading only the introduction and discussion sections of the paper seems so efficient—a little background followed by an erudite discussion of the results.

Do not be fooled! We have every right to pin our own interpretation on the results. The burden of proof is upon the authors to convince us that they are right. The whole purpose of the exercise of critical reading is to provide clinicians with skills to analyze the article and make an independent assessment of whether it is worthy. It is a matter of educating the palate.

But a word of caution! Because it is much easier to reject an article as unsound than to give it unqualified praise, it is easy to become cynical about interpreting medical articles. If we look hard and long enough, we are bound to find some blemishes in the best of reported studies. For the reader, the task is to acknowledge human imperfection and decide whether, given the limitations of almost any study, the net effect of the work is useful and valid. In the final analysis, can we believe the results? Is the work applicable to our clinic operation or the kinds of patients we see?

Bear in mind through the next chapters that, although the pitfalls associated with designing and executing medical studies seem numerous and the apparent defects in published works many, there is much valuable information waiting to be chewed and digested.

References

1. ADLER, M. J. *How to Read a Book: The Art of Getting a Liberal Education.* New York: Simon and Schuster, 1940.

2. ASHKENAZI, A., LEVIN, S., IDAR, D., OR, A., ROSENBERG, I., AND HANDZEL, Z. T. In vitro cell-mediated immunologic assay for cow's milk allergy. *Pediatrics* 65:399–402, 1980.

3. BECK, A. M., LORING, H., AND LOCKWOOD, R. The ecology of dog bite injury in St. Louis, Missouri. *Public Health Rep.* 90:262–267, 1975.

4. BECKER, M. H., DRACHMAN, R. H., AND KIRSCHT, J. P. A field experiment to evaluate various outcomes of continuity of physician care. *Am. J. Public Health* 64:1062–1070, 1974.

5. BISSET, G. S., GAUM, W., AND KAPLAN, S. The ice bag: A new technique for interruption of supraventricular tachycardia. *J. Pediatr.* 97:593–595, 1980.

6. CAMPBELL, D. T. AND STANLEY, J. C. *Experimental and Quasi-experimental Designs for Research.* Chicago: Rand McNally, 1966.

7. CRAWFORD, G., BRANCATO, F., AND HOLMES, K. K. Streptococcal pharyngitis: Diagnosis by Gram stain. *Ann. Intern. Med.* 90:293–297, 1979.

8. DAVIS, J. P., CHESNEY, P. J., WAND, P. J., LAVENTURE, M., AND THE INVESTIGATION AND LABORATORY TEAM. Toxic-shock syndrome: Epidemiologic features, recurrence, risk factors and prevention. *N. Engl. J. Med.* 303:1429–1435, 1980.

9. EDIDIN, D. V., LEVITSKY, L. L., SCHEY, W., DUMBOVIC, N., AND CAMPOS, A. Resurgence of nutritional rickets associated with breast-feeding and special dietary practices. *Pediatrics* 65:232–235, 1980.

10. GILLENWATER, J. Y., HARRISON, R. B., AND KUNIN, C. M. Natural history of bacteriuria in schoolgirls. *N. Engl. J. Med.* 301:396–399, 1979.

11. HAYNES, R. B., SACKETT, D. L., TAYLOR, D. W., GIBSON, E. S., AND JOHNSON, A. L. Increased absenteeism from work after detection and labeling of hypertensive patients. *N. Engl. J. Med.* 299:741–744, 1978.

12. KASS, E. H. Antimicrobial drug use in general hospitals in Pennsylvania. *Ann. Intern. Med.* 89:800–801, 1978.

13. KESSLER, I. I. AND CLARK, J. P. Saccharin, cyclamate, and human bladder cancer: No evidence of association. *JAMA* 240:349–355, 1978.

14. KIRBY, B. D., SNYDER, K. M., MEYER, R. D., AND FEINGOLD, S. M. Legionnaires' disease: Clinical features of 24 cases. *Ann. Intern. Med.* 89:297–309, 1978.

15. MADDREY, W. C. AND BOITNOTT, J. K. Isoniazid hepatitis. *Ann. Intern. Med.* 79:1–12, 1973.

16. MCGOWAN, J. E., JR., BRATTON, L., KLEIN, J. O., AND FINLAND, M. Bacteremia in febrile children seen in a "walk-in" pediatric clinic. *N. Engl. J. Med.* 288:1309–1312, 1973.

17. MOSS, T. J., DELAND, E. C., AND MALONEY, J. V. Selection of medical students for graduate training: Pass/fail versus grades. *N. Engl. J. Med.* 299:25–27, 1978.

18. OCKENE, I. S., SHAY, M, J., ALPERT, J. S., WEINER, B. H., AND DALEN, J. E. Unexplained chest pain in patients with normal coronary arteriograms: A follow-up study of functional status. *N. Engl. J. Med.* 303:1249–1252, 1980.

19. OSTERHOLM, M. T., FORFANG, J. C., RISTINEN, T. L., ET AL. An outbreak of foodborne giardiasis. *N. Engl. J. Med.* 304:24–28, 1981.

20. PAUL, R. H. AND HON, E. H. Clinical fetal monitoring. V. Effect on perinatal outcome. *Am. J. Obstet. Gynecol.* 118:529–533, 1974.

21. PRIEBE, H. J., SKILLMAN, J. J., BUSHNELL, L. S., LONG, P. C., AND SILEN, W. Antacid versus cimetidine in preventing acute gastrointestinal bleeding: A randomized trial in 75 critically ill patients. *N. Engl. J. Med.* 302:426–430, 1980.

TWO

Study Design: General Considerations

I'll no more on't: it hath made me mad.
—Hamlet, Act III, Scene I

Although Hamlet may not have been specifically discussing his feelings on the taxonomy of study designs, he could well have been. Sorting through the maze of terms that are commonly employed to describe the design of studies could totter the stablest mind or flutter the stoutest heart. We are likely to encounter references to retrospective and prospective studies, prevalence, case-control and cohort studies, follow-up, and cross-sectional and trohoc studies. There are prolective and retrolective studies. Along with longitudinal studies and incidence studies, there are experimental studies and clinical trials. We even get combinations such as retrospective cohort studies. The list goes on, but at this point most readers are ready to throw their hands skyward in irrevocable despair. How did we arrive at such a confusing state of affairs and what can a relatively reasonable soul expect to gain from making some sense of the taxonomy of study design?

Epidemiologists are probably most to blame for the glut of terminology. As methodologists they are rightfully concerned with precise definitions of the tools of their trade. Unfortunately, no one in the union seems able to accept the definitions of other members, and the neologisms have sprouted. One article in an epidemiology journal describes and discusses twenty-three definitions of the word "epidemiology" [10]. Alas, as is the case with new cars and cold

17

remedies, the proliferation of terms describing study designs suggests that none is entirely satisfactory.

Although it is tempting for the clinician to leave this semantic tangle to those who enjoy it, there are several principles about study design that the intelligent reader needs to master. The trick is to keep the forest in view without floundering in the foliage. Identifying the structure of a study gives the reader a jump in assessing the validity of an article. Just as knowing the make and model of an automobile suggests predictive features about its gas mileage, repair record, and comfort, classifying a study provides insight about strengths to be anticipated and weaknesses to probe for.

Let us begin with an overview to put the elements of study design into perspective. For purposes of the discussion we will not haggle about terminology. The goal is to get at the concepts that underlie designs. Table 2–1 supplies a schematic of the basic designs into which most medical studies fall. A large number of reports in the literature can be designated as descriptive as seen on the left hand side of the table.

Descriptive Studies

As the term suggests, descriptive articles serve chiefly to record events, observations, and activities. They do not provide detailed explanations for the cause of disease or offer the kind of evidence we need to evaluate the efficacy of a new treatment. They are, however, invaluable documentaries that, once filed, may lead to exciting discoveries. At its least complicated, a descriptive study is a report of a case or a small series of cases that an observer feels should be brought to the attention of colleagues. Describing an unusual episode of poisoning or an atypical rash developing after administration of a new medication are examples of descriptive studies at their simplest. These reports alert clinicians about possible drug side effects, unusual complications of illnesses, or surprising presentations of diseases. Caution must always be exercised in interpreting a single report or series of cases, since it is not always clear that the unusual rash or ringing in the ears reported by the patient given a new antibiotic is related to the drug; however, the observations first noted in descriptive studies often lead to further confirmatory work that produces important findings.

Table 2-1 Basic Study Designs

EXPLANATORY

Examine etiology, cause, efficacy using the strategy of comparisons

DESCRIPTIVE

Document and communicate experience: share ideas, programs, treatments, unusual events and observations
Begin search for explanations

Examples:

Case report or series
- Rash developing while on drug
- Cluster of cases of vaginal cancer

Clinical series
- Treatment of 50 snakebite victims

Population
- Diagnoses seen in family practice
- Community survey of needs of elderly

Program or course
- Medical-student course on sexuality

EXPERIMENTAL

Evaluate efficacy of therapeutic, educational, administrative interventions
Investigator controls allocation

Examples:

Clinical trial
- Compare two antidepressant drugs
- Surgical vs. medical management of angina

Educational intervention
- Self-instruction vs. lecture on anemia

Health-care trial
- Nurse practitioner vs. physician care

OBSERVATIONAL

Seek causes, etiologies predictors, better diagnosis
Investigator observes nature

Examples:

Case-control
- Diets of toxemic vs. nontoxemic patients

Follow-up
- Development of renal complications in school girls with bacteriuria

Cross-sectional
- Prevalence of bacteremia in febrile children

Case reports have been around for a long time. Consider William Heberden's 1772 account of chest pain occurring in "nearly a hundred people" [5].

> There is a disorder of the breast marked with strong and peculiar symptoms, considerable for the kind of danger belonging to it, and not extremely rare . . . They who are afflicted with it, are seized while they are walking, (more especially if it be up hill, and soon after eating) with a painful and most disagreeable sensation in the breast which seems as if it would extinguish life, if it were to increase or to continue; but the moment they stand still, all this uneasiness vanishes. . . . In some inveterate cases it has been brought on by the motion of a horse, or a carriage, and even by swallowing, coughing, going to stool, or speaking, or any disturbance of mind.

This elegant description turns out to be the first delineation of the syndrome of angina pectoris.

More recently, a Boston physician named Herbst described the occurrence of an unusual form of cancer among seven young women patients [7]. This initial report of a series of cases of adenocarcinoma of the vagina led to further, explanatory studies that elucidated the relationship between maternal intake of diethylstilbestrol and subsequent development of this rare disease in female offspring [6, 8].

Another type of useful descriptive study is the clinical series in which a physician describes the outcome of 100 patients undergoing a new technique for snaring gallstones or how 50 snake-bite victims were treated—not fancy research, but useful catalogs of the experience of others.

Large populations can also be the subject of descriptive studies. Collecting diagnostic information on a practice population by counting the number of hypertensives, diabetics, and acute sore throats seen over a period of time has been used for "defining the content of family practice" [11]. This type of information helps to make practice-management decisions, such as, assessing the need for a dietician to counsel diabetics or planning a curriculum for training residents. Describing a new course in human sexuality that has been successfully taught to medical students or conducting a community survey to assess the health needs of the geriatric population are other examples that use this type of design. So in addition to being starting points for more elaborate assaults on the etiology of disease, descriptive studies can be used for a variety of educational, administrative, and health-planning purposes.

The major limitation of the descriptive study is that it does not provide explanations, offer causes, or supply evidence that one treatment is superior to another. The design lacks an essential ingredient—the use of comparisons—to do this. This fundamental shortcoming is nicely illustrated by a chapter from the angina pectoris story that was begun by Heberden's descriptive work. Therapy for this disabling condition has been an ongoing medical challenge. In the 1950s, a new surgical technique was developed that appeared to hold great promise for angina sufferers. The theory was that tieing off the internal mammary arteries would force into use collateral blood vessels that ultimately would increase the blood supply to the myocardium. Several case-series describing this surgery were reported, including a large group of patients from Pennsylvania [9]. The results were most encouraging. Of some 50 patients who had the operation, two-thirds noted subjective improvement of their angina two to six months following the operation. It was noted, however, that investigators were unable to document "objective evidence of improvement by electrocardiogram that matched their rates of subjective relief." Undismayed, the authors concluded,

> We believe that when the patient feels better, is able to return to productive occupations, and lives a more normal life, he is improved. There is no machine available today to document these improvements other than the old-fashioned history of the case. In the evaluation of coronary disease . . . time is the only measure which will give true answers. It is evident to us that evaluation of this surgical procedure will have to be based on a formula involving large numbers of patients and much time leavened by careful follow-up and history taking [12].

Unfortunately, a crucial ingredient was missing in this optimistic assessment; no comparison group had been included. For although angina has a physiological basis—anoxic pain coming in response to inadequate blood supply—the disabling discomfort is largely subjective. There is always the possibility that patients who are desperate for relief will respond favorably to any procedure offered them. This descriptive effort, regardless of the number of patients it includes, cannot separate effects of the operation on arterial blood flow from its potent power of suggestion.

An ingenious experiment was devised to assess the possibility of this placebo effect. Cobb and colleagues gathered a group of 17 patients whom they felt were candidates for internal mammary ligation [2]. All patients were taken to the operating room and had the initial stages of the operation, including chest-wall incisions, performed. However, only one-half of the patients actually had their mammary arteries tied off. In the evaluation that followed the operation, it was found that among the most dramatic cures were those patients who had the sham operations. No important difference in improvement of angina symptoms could be demonstrated between the two groups. In fact, patients who had not had their arteries ligated tended to show more favorable results with respect to decreased use of nitroglycerin and increased exercise capacity. This is a dramatic example of the need for comparisons in clinical studies.

Explanatory Studies

Comparison is the basic strategy of explanatory studies. Such studies seek answers to questions: Which treatment for breast cancer is most effective? Is there a relationship between use of oral hypoglycemics and heart disease? What are the factors that predict which patients will miss appointments? Explanatory studies attempt to provide insight into etiology or find better treatments. The methods employed can be grouped into two major approaches as seen on the right-hand side of table 2–1.

Experimental Studies

The first of the explanatory study designs is the experimental strategy which is familiar to most of us from undergraduate chemistry or psychology. In medical research it travels under the aliases of the controlled trial, clinical trial, health-care trial, or intervention trial. The primary feature that distinguishes the controlled trial from other explanatory studies is the active intervention of the investigator. The researcher gives an antidepressant medication to one group of volunteers and a placebo to another group; one-half of a medical-school class is selected to receive a new self-instructional package on anemia while the other one-half gets a lecture; patients in

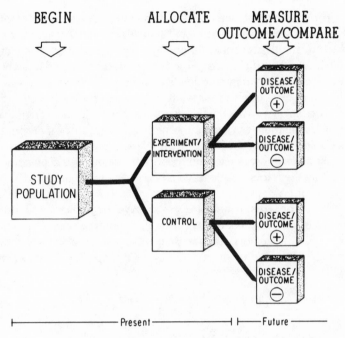

Figure 2-1. Experimental or controlled trial design.

a practice are randomly assigned to a physician or to a nurse practitioner for care. In each case, the researcher who is testing the efficacy of the method is able to exercise control by assigning subjects to medications, lectures, or nurse practitioners. Figure 2-1 illustrates the general outline of the controlled trial. It is an extremely important form of study design and will be dealt with in more detail later.

Observational Studies

Observational studies also utilize comparisons to examine and explain medical mysteries. However, unlike the controlled trial, the observational study relegates researchers to the role of bystanders. They study the natural course of health events, gather data about subjects, and classify and sort them. By the strategy of making comparisons, they then try to provide insights into the cause of diseases.

The plethora of terms at the beginning of this chapter notwithstanding, there are really only two fundamental ways of approaching an observational study. We can start by studying individuals who already have a particular disease or outcome (patients with toxemia of pregnancy or low satisfaction with medical care, or doctors who have become surgeons) and search for some factors in their past that may explain the outcome. Figure 2–2 outlines this approach. Alternatively, we can begin with a group of individuals who do not yet have the outcome of interest, examine and classify them by characteristics we think might be related to the outcome, and follow them to see who develops disease (*see* figure 2–3).

The Case-Control Design. We begin with the outcome—toxemia, low patient satisfaction, or surgical specialty—and look for features of people who share that outcome. Do they eat too much salt, spend more time in the waiting room, or have excep-

Figure 2–2. Case-control design.

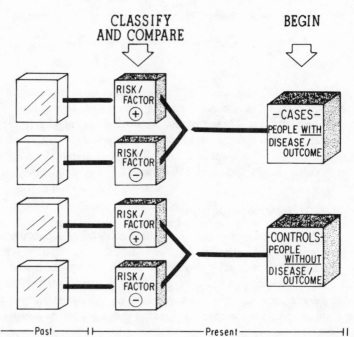

CLASSIFY AND COMPARE   BEGIN

RISK / FACTOR ⊕

RISK / FACTOR ⊖

–CASES–
PEOPLE WITH DISEASE / OUTCOME

RISK / FACTOR ⊕

RISK / FACTOR ⊖

–CONTROLS–
PEOPLE WITHOUT DISEASE / OUTCOME

———Past——— ———Present———

BEGIN   MEASURE/CLASSIFY   MEASURE
                                      OUTCOME/COMPARE

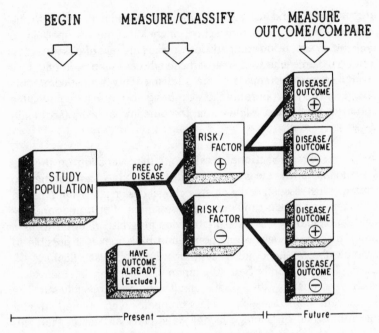

Figure 2-3. Follow-up design.

tionally high personal motivation when compared with people who are not toxemic, dissatisfied, or surgeons? If differences in frequencies of the characteristics between the cases and the comparison group are found, we have made a positive step toward explaining the illness. We will call this the case-control approach although it should be clear from the examples used that the term "case" is used broadly to define an individual who already has the outcome of interest. That outcome need not be a medical disease. The term "case-control" does convey the major activity of the design: that we begin at the end with people who have the outcome and compare their characteristics with subjects who do not.

Follow-Up Design. We begin with people who have not yet experienced the outcome: prenatal patients early in pregnancy, new registrants in a practice, or third-year medical students. Characteristics of the group, such as diet, waiting time, or motivation, are measured and catalogued, and the researcher sits back and watches for toxemia, dissatisfaction, or choice of medical specialty to develop. Again, using comparisons, such as the rate of dissatisfaction among patients who wait against those who are seen promptly, light is shed on possible causes of the outcome. This is most commonly referred to as the cohort or follow-up design because it begins with a cohort or group and follows it till the outcome appears (*see* figure 2–3).

Cross-Sectional Design. A third variation on the observational study is the *cross-sectional* approach. A blend of the two strategies just discussed, the cross-sectional design takes a population or cohort and makes simultaneous assessment of outcomes and potential predictors. This slice-of-time design is also referred to as a prevalence study because its population basis makes it possible to estimate the frequency of disease within a group (*see* figure 2–4). During the last month, 5 of 20 women who eat high salt diets were toxemic compared with 3 of 50 patients who consume little salt. The 17 percent of medical-school-class graduates who entered surgical internships had on average higher National Board scores than students going to pediatric programs.

A Concocted Example

For purposes of illustration, we can take a single example and try out each of the major explanatory approaches. To give us a working terminology, we will call them experimental, case-control, and follow-up designs.

The Problem. During the past few years of practice we have made a fascinating clinical observation. In talking to patients who wear glasses and suffer from poor visual acuity we have noted that their diets seem to be remarkably deficient in carrots. Now everyone knows that the carotenes that give carrots their lovely orange glow are essential for formation of rhodopsin, a retinal pigment associated with good night vision, but it appears we are on to the illuminating discovery that previously unappreciated components of carrots may actually aid visual acuity. In fact, our first informal survey revealed that of five bespectacled patients queried, all admitted to a singular disinterest in carrots. The question is how to pursue

BEGIN   MEASURE/CLASSIFY
              AND COMPARE

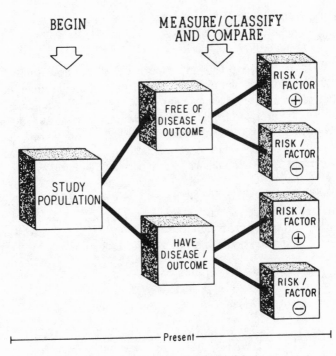

Figure 2-4. *Cross-sectional design.*

this exciting hunch and create an explanatory study that will substantiate our hypothesis that an association exists between good vision and carrot consumption.

Case-Control Design. We begin by collecting 100 of our spectacle-wearing patients to represent the cases. They already have the outcome—poor visual acuity. As a comparison or control group, we identify another 100 individuals—patients who are generally like our first group except that they enjoy 20/20 vision. We then proceed to ask each of these 200 people to give us an exhaustive accounting of their dietary habits over recent years, paying particular attention to their consumption of carrots. Our hope will be that a conspicuous difference in carrot-eating will be found between those with good and those with poor vision. If the patients with poor vision are well below the comparison group with respect to carrot intake, we will have evidence to support the link between carrots and eyesight. Figure 2–5 reflects all this.

Follow-Up Design. Figure 2–6 shows how a follow-up study might look for our example. All patients who enter the practice will be given a test for visual acuity. Subjects who already have poor acuity will be dropped from further consideration. They already have the outcome. For the remainder, those with good vision, dietary records will be maintained so we will have an accurate account of the carrot intake of all our subjects. These people will be followed for the next ten years and at the end of that time everyone's vision will be retested. Armed with information on carrot consumption with which to classify subjects, we will be able to compare the vision status of patients with high intake with those who eat few or no carrots at all. If carrot eaters see better than those who eschew the orange roots,

Figure 2–5. Case-control design.

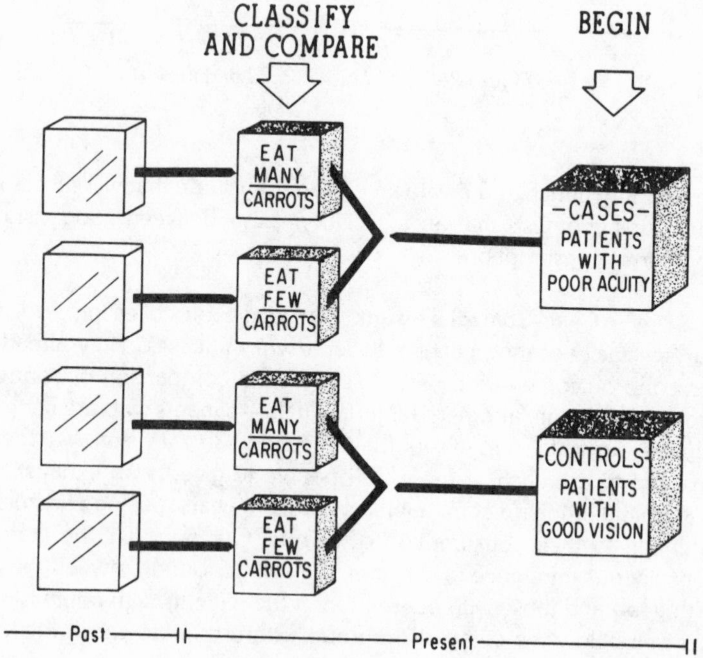

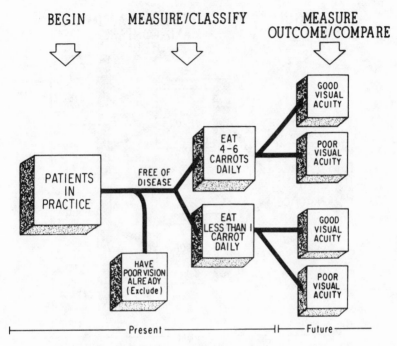

BEGIN   MEASURE/CLASSIFY   MEASURE OUTCOME/COMPARE

Figure 2-6. Follow-up design.

our hypothesis will be supported. It should be emphasized that this follow-up design just described is an observational rather than experimental study despite the fact that as investigators we seemed to be assuming a very active role. We examined eyesight and counted carrots, but we never told our patients how many carrots they should eat. That was left to nature.

On the way to performing our follow-up study we dismissed the portion of our population who were screened and found lacking in visual acuity. We could have gained some information from this group, however. Had we taken the trouble to ask them about their current carrot-eating habits, we could have compared their intake with the carrot consumption of patients with good eyesight. This slice of information from our practice would be a cross-sectional study: Do patients with good vision eat more carrots than those with poor vision? *(see figure 2-7)*. Like the case-control study, information on diet is from the past, albeit the immediate past. Unlike the case-

BEGIN   MEASURE/CLASSIFY
                       AND COMPARE

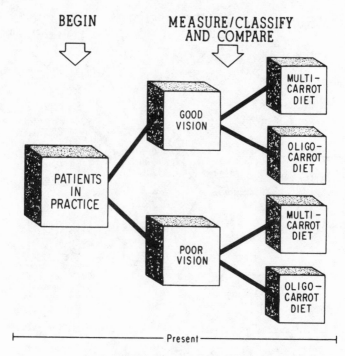

Figure 2-7.   Cross-sectional design.

control design, however, the study begins with a large practice population instead of selected cases. Classifying patients by both carrot consumption and vision, we learn the prevalence of low acuity in the practice and get an estimate of the role that carrot eating contributes to deficient vision.

Experimental Design. We again begin with a group of patients who are free of the outcome, that is, have good vision (*see* figure 2-8). We divide our population into two groups. To the first we offer a special diet including everything from carrot daiquiris to carrot cake. In the diet of the second group, carrots and their by-products are avoided. During the months and years that follow, we diligently perform vision examinations to see how our two groups fare and ultimately compare the high and low carrot diet groups with respect to vision outcomes.

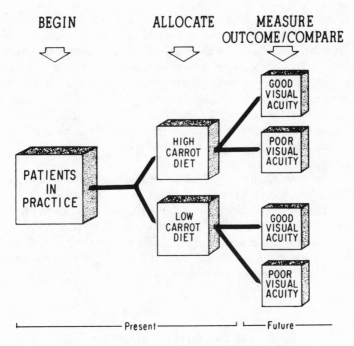

BEGIN   ALLOCATE   MEASURE
                              OUTCOME/COMPARE

Figure 2-8. *Experimental or controlled trial design.*

Each of these strategies has a distinctive flavor. The case-control format has an economy about it, but one can sense difficulties in retrieving information from the past and in finding proper groups to compare. The follow-up and experimental designs allow better planning and control but require ongoing diligence to keep track of subjects and see that people stay on their diets. We will examine the advantages of the different methodologies as well as explore their limitations and tribulations in the next few chapters.

A Real Example

Herbst's work on adenocarcinoma of the vagina, which was discussed as an example of a descriptive work, demonstrates nicely how a single topic may be studied using several different designs. Following his initial report of the seven cases of cancer, Herbst set about explaining his observation by means of a case-control study

[8]. By that time, he had uncovered an eighth case of the unusual tumor. For each of these cases, he found four young women who were born at about the same time and did not have the disease. He compared a host of factors between these cases of cancer and their controls, including everything from birthweight, history of tonsillectomy, and presence of household pets to use of cosmetics, cigarettes, and alcohol. The finding that leapt out of all these comparisons was that mothers of seven out of eight of the cases had used stilbestrol during pregnancy compared to none of the 32 controls. The link was established!

From that point Herbst went on to perform a follow-up investigation on some 800 pregnancies that were treated in a stilbestrol clinic in Boston [6]. By tracking the female offspring of as many of these women as he could find and comparing them with the group of young women who were born at about the same time but whose mothers were not given stilbestrol, he was able to obtain tissue diagnoses from the genital tract that supported his hypothesis.

More Confusing Terminology

Identifying study designs can be a perplexing business. Even people who ought to know better occasionally get caught with their terms in a tangle. Bits of jargon that are particularly troublesome are the duos: cases and controls, and prospective and retrospective. The ambiguous use of these terms accounts for much confusion, pain, and suffering.

Cases and Controls

Take, for example, an article that gives itself simultaneous billing as a "long-term case-control study," and an account of the "natural history of bacteriuria in school-girls" [4]. Now pause and reflect. A study tracking the natural history of something sounds like it ought to be following a group of subjects with a certain characteristic for a period of time to see what happens to them. It does not sound like a case-control design that starts with people who have an outcome and tries to discover past habits that may be related. Sure enough, in this study the investigators evaluated a group of 60 schoolgirls who were found through a screening program to have bacteriuria, then reexamined them periodically for a number of years to see who developed renal complications. Complication rates for girls who had bacteriuria were found to be substantially higher when compared with rates for a group of girls who were without infections. A perfect example of a follow-up study!

The confusion arises because of the use of the term "case" to describe girls who have bacteriuria. They are indeed cases as the clinician uses the term to identify patients who have a disease. They are not cases, however, in the sense the researcher uses the term to define a group with an outcome that will serve as a starting point for a comparative study. Bacteriuria is not the outcome of this observational study. The outcome is chronic renal disease. Bacteriuria is a characteristic shared by a portion of the initial cohort of schoolgirls that we wish to follow. At the same time, controls as used in this paper are really a subset of girls from a larger population who were screened for urinary-tract infection and found free of bacteriuria. They are followed forward in time for comparative purposes and assessed for renal complications. They are not the foils in a case-control design.

To quibble with Gertrude Stein a bit—a case is not a case is not a case. Sometimes a case is a subject in a specific explanatory strategy who has been chosen because she has the outcome under study—toxemia, low satisfaction, or poor visual acuity. Sometimes that same toxemia, low satisfaction, or poor visual acuity is the starting point of the study and groups of cases that share a characteristic are watched for development of outcomes, such as perinatal death, broken appointments, or traffic accidents. Readers must avoid the temptation to classify every article that refers to cases and controls as a case-control study. It may be a follow-up or experimental design.

Prospective and Retrospective

Perhaps the most confusing of all terminology encountered in descriptions of medical studies are references to prospective and retrospective designs. It does not take an etymologist to tell you that these two words describe a relationship to time—looking forward in time and looking backward. Unfortunately, in common medical usage they have also come to be synonyms for design structures. Studies we call case-control designs are also known as retrospective studies; those that we designate as cohort or follow-up studies are also referred to as prospective studies.

Time can be a bugbear unless readers keep the time frame in which a study is conducted separate from the strategy of comparison that is being used. Retrospective studies begin and end in the present but involve a major backward glance to collect information about events that occurred in the past. Prospective studies also begin in the present but march forward, collecting data about a population whose outcome lies in the future. But these two terms do not offer sufficient precision about the strategy of the study. It should be clear, for example, that both the controlled trial and the follow-up design proceed in a prospective, forward fashion. Both these strategies begin with a population, gather measurements, and watch for developments in the future, but conceptually experimental versus observational strategies are very different.

Similarly, the notion that any study that uses data which are collected retrospectively falls into the case-control category is misleading. One design that is becoming increasingly popular utilizes the follow-up technique but does it using information from the past. This strategy labors under the awkward designations of retrospective follow-up, historical prospective, or nonconcurrent follow-up design. The key to the success of this approach (as diagrammed in figure 2–9) is the availability of carefully kept records from the past.

Researchers wishing to examine the relationship between alcohol consumption and development of high blood pressure might need to wait twenty years before patients they have screened and classified with respect to alcohol consumption develop high blood pressure. If, however, they can find medical records that document the drinking habits and blood pressures of people fifteen to twenty years ago, they can greatly condense the time frame of the study. They select a cohort of people whose alcohol consumption was conscientiously recorded in 1960, follow them up to the present by measuring current blood pressures, and produce a retrospective-prospective, or retrospective follow-up study.

Sartwell [12], Feinstein [3], and Clark and Hopkins [1] have written in some detail about the confusion resulting from mixing connotations of time with references to design strategy. It is best for purposes of clarity to reduce prospective and retrospective to their roles as clock-watchers and employ more precise terms to describe study plans.

BEGIN   MEASURE/CLASSIFY   MEASURE
                                         OUTCOME/COMPARE

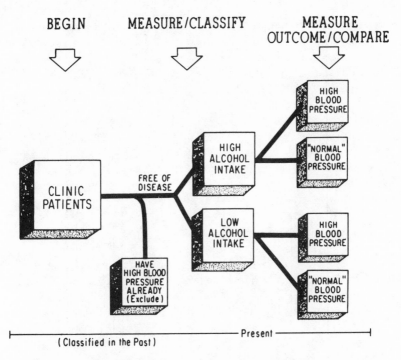

Figure 2-9. Retrospective follow-up design.

Table 2-2 attempts to place the terminology chaos in some order. In it, designs have been grouped into categories that should be most useful for clinical readers. Terms we will be using head the lists with synonyms or relatives in approach and intent grouped below. Some may object to such insensitive lumping of so large a number of elegant terms. Indeed, there are some fine distinctions within the groupings that have been passed over. The terminology used to describe experimental studies, for example, has expanded to encompass the increasing variety of topics that the design has come to address. "Clinical trials" suggests a subject matter confined to evaluating therapeutic maneuvers with traditional clinical outcomes like relief of angina or improved survival. Health-care trials, it is argued by Spitzer et al. [13], evaluate a broader range of health outcomes including "personal, sociologic, administrative, and economic data that are seldom considered in conventional biomedical

Table 2-2   The Terminology of Study Designs

DESCRIPTIVE

- Case reports
- Case series
- Clinical series

EXPLANATORY

EXPERIMENTAL

Controlled trial
- Clinical trial
- Health-care trial
- Intervention trial

OBSERVATIONAL

Case-Control
- Retrospective
- Case-referent
- Case-compere
- Trohoc

Follow-up
- Cohort
- Incidence
- Prospective
- Longitudinal

Retrospective follow-up
- Historical prospective
- Retrospective cohort
- Nonconcurrent follow-up

Cross-sectional
- Prevalence

research." They cite as examples the trials comparing the use of nurse practitioners with physicians in medical settings or trials of patient-education programs designed to improve compliance. The term "intervention trial" has also been used to imply the broadened scope of the methodology. Nuances notwithstanding, all share a common controlled, experimental approach.

Feinstein has found that case-control and cohort do not satisfy his needs and has put forth detailed arguments for use of terms like "trohoc," "prolective" and "retrolective" [3].

Summary

Having gone through the strenuous exercise of pinning a label on the structure of a study, what reward can we expect for the effort? The next three chapters will burrow deeper into the problems of design and, hopefully, come out with useful advice for assessing the strengths and weaknesses of common designs. To put the study into a methodological category ask the following:

1. Is the design a descriptive or explanatory effort? Is the author simply detailing an experience with cases, practices, or treatments or making comparisons in hopes of establishing etiologies or evaluating interventions?

2. If comparisons are being made, is the investigator observing the course of events or creating an experiment by assigning subjects to receive a pill, an exercise program, or a piece of health advice.

3. If the design is observational, are cases who already have a disease or outcome compared with unaffected controls for preexisting characteristics? Or do investigators classify and follow a cohort of subjects for development of the outcome or effect of interest?

References

1. CLARK, V. A. AND HOPKINS, C. E. Time is of the essence. *J. Chron. Dis.* 20:565–569, 1967.

2. COBB, L. A., THOMAS, G. I., DILLARD, D. H., MERENDINO, K. A., AND BRUCE, R. A. An evaluation of internal-mammary-artery ligation by a double-blind technique. *N. Engl. J. Med.* 260:1115–1118, 1959.

3. FEINSTEIN, A. R. *Clinical Biostatistics*. St. Louis, Mo.: C. V. Mosby Co. 1977.

4. GILLENWATER, J. Y., HARRISON, R. B., AND KUNIN, C. M. Natural history of bacteriuria in schoolgirls. A long-term case-control study. *N. Engl. J. Med.* 301:396–399, 1979.

5. HEBERDEN, W. Commentaries on the history and cure of diseases. In F. A. Willius and T. E. Keys (Eds.). *Classics of Cardiology*. Vol. 1. New York: Dover Publications Inc., 1961.

6. HERBST, A. L., POSKANZER, D. C., ROBBOY, S. J., FRIEDLANDER, L., AND SCULLY, R. E. Prenatal exposure to stilbestrol: A prospective comparison of exposed female offspring with unexposed controls. *N. Engl. J. Med.* 292:334–339, 1975.

7. HERBST, A. L. AND SCULLY, R. E. Adenocarcinoma of the vagina in adolescence: A report of 7 cases including 6 clear-cell carcinomas (so-called mesonephromas). *Cancer* 25:745–757, 1970.

8. HERBST, A. L., ULFELDER, H., AND POSKANZER, D. C. Adenocarcinoma of the vagina: Association of maternal stilbestrol therapy with tumor appearance in young women. *N. Engl. J. Med.* 284:878–881, 1971.

9. KITCHELL, J. R., GLOVER, R. P., AND KYLE, R. H. Bilateral internal mammary artery ligation for angina pectoris. *Am. J. Cardiol.* 1:46–50, 1958. Reprinted with permission.

10. LILIENFELD, D. E. Definitions of epidemiology. *Am. J. Epidemiol.* 107:87–90, 1978.

11. MARSLAND, D. W., WOOD, M., AND MAYO, F. Content of family practice. *J. Fam. Pract.* 3:37–68, 1976.

12. SARTWELL, P. E. Retrospective studies: A review for the clinician. *Ann. Intern. Med.* 81:381–386, 1974.

13. SPITZER, W. O., FEINSTEIN, A. R., AND SACKETT, D. L. What is a health care trial? *JAMA* 233:161–163, 1975.

THREE

Study Design:
The Case-Control
Approach

*. . . you yourself sir, should be as old as I am if, like a crab,
you could go backward.*
—Hamlet, Act II, Scene II

Case-control studies have been much maligned. Who
among us has not experienced the dismay of making a particularly
bright remark referencing Dr. Rasputin's work on hemophilia, only to
hear ourselves rebuffed by the ultimate put-down, "Of course those
were retrospective studies." The implication is clear. Nothing could
be a cruder masquerade for a research study than a retrospective or
case-control effort. It is surprising how common this notion is. Some
people continue to argue that satisfactory solutions to research questions can never be obtained through the case-control methodology
because there are insurmountable problems in going backward.

It is well to clear our heads now of sweeping prejudices against
the case-control design. For although the method falls prey to a
number of difficulties, an increasing number of studies are being
performed this way. Cole reports a four- to seven-fold increase in the
number of case-control reports published in *Lancet* over the 20-year
period from 1956–1976 [4]. During this same time, the *American
Journal of Epidemiology* also showed an increase in the use of the
design among its published articles. With the rising costs of performing long-term, follow-up studies on large populations, the case-

control design will probably find even greater use in the future. The method has some very compelling features that should be recognized before we start going after the tender points.

Advantages of the Case-Control Design

The case-control design is ideally suited for initial, explanatory ventures. As we have seen with Herbst's observations on vaginal carcinoma [7,8] or the example of carrots and vision, many important medical discoveries begin with a clinical observation or hunch. An unusual clustering of cases of cancer is noted, a surprising side effect is observed following the use of an antibiotic, a group of children with learning disabilities are reported to be formula fed as infants. The handiest way to see if these hunches lead to valid discoveries is to make some quick comparisons with subjects who are readily at hand. Are patients with mesothelioma more likely to have been exposed to asbestos than a comparison group? Is enterocolitis truly higher among patients receiving clindamycin than other antibiotics? Is there a difference in the history of breast and bottle feeding between children with learning disabilities and those who perform well in school? The case-control design is ideal for trying these hypotheses. It is very *efficient*. Since our novel observations generally begin with patients who have experienced the unusual disease or side effect, collecting cases is relatively easy. Hospitals and outpatient clinics are replete with patients who already have diseases or outcomes we may wish to study. We need not wait years for the outcome to develop nor expend great energy tracking down subjects who require follow-up.

Another widely advertised advantage of the case-control design is its *utility for studying rare diseases*. This point certainly appears to have merit since even the most common diseases occur relatively infrequently. The incidence of breast cancer, for example, is about 85 per 100,000 women; only about one in 100 men between 50 and 59 years of age will have a heart attack each year. This means that to perform follow-up studies extremely large populations must be monitored to supply even a small handful of cases.

A less well-publicized but compelling point in favor of the case-control design is an *ethical* one. There are areas of inquiry where neither experimental nor follow-up observational studies can be sanctioned. Take for example the question of the relationship between childhood lead poisoning and mental-retardation syndromes. It has been known for a number of years that children who ingest lead-based paint are at risk of developing acute lead poisoning. This devastating illness, characterized by convulsions, encephalopathy, and permanent brain damage has prompted extensive public-health programs to detect and treat children who eat lead paint. As many children were screened for evidence of increased lead absorption, it was noted that there were children who had excessive amounts of lead in their bodies but who had no obvious symptoms. The question arose whether these children might have some subtle, subclinical manifestations of neurologic impairment as a result of chronic low-level heavy-metal poisoning. Important as this medical problem is, it is apparent that the methods of investigation available to study the problem are limited. An experimental design is out of the question. No one would dream of deliberately exposing children to lead paint to see if toxic manifestations develop, but observational, follow-up studies are no more tenable. To do a proper follow-up study would require measuring and categorizing childrens' exposure to lead paint then following them to see who develops hyperactivity or low I.Q. Although this design does not involve the intentional manipulation of an experimental trial, it would require investigators to observe children who were exposed to a potential toxin without intervening. Almost as bad! A problem like this can only be studied by asking about prior exposure to lead. A retrospective follow-up design might be an option if information happens to be available from past records about a child's development and habits. However, for the most part, any investigator wishing to study exposure to an agent of known toxicity, like lead, must be satisfied with the case-control design.

Problems of Case-Control Designs

Adequacy of Information

Although it saves a great deal of time to be able to glance backward in time over a cancer patient's 20-year smoking history or a hypertensive's lifetime intake of salt, there is a risk that the records of the past may not contain sufficient detail for the purposes of the present. It may be important to know about a patient's previous weight or blood pressure or serum cholesterol. If that information has not been recorded by some clairvoyant in anticipation of its future utility, we are out of luck. This is the hobgoblin of research that relies on using medical records. Even when needed information is available, it is often of questionable reliability since standardized techniques for collecting data may not have been practiced. It is particularly important that information obtained from records of cases and controls be of comparable quality and completeness. Unfortunately, this is not always the situation. Studies such as those attempting to relate the use of estrogens in postmenopausal women to the development of endometrial cancer are plagued by this problem. Women who have cancer and have taken replacement estrogens have generally had extensive contact with the medical profession. That's how they got put on estrogens. They're likely to have had increased contact with doctors during the time preceding their diagnosis because of symptoms from the undetected disease. This means that from the medical record point of view these cases are likely to have more detailed information about use of medication and other health information than are most groups of women with whom they may be compared.

Biased Recall

Many case-comparison studies rely not on medical records but on information supplied by the subjects themselves. This creates a special kind of problem that is a danger to interpretation. It is called biased or selective recall. Biased recall means, in essence, that people who have unpleasant diseases may recall the past quite differently from any comparison, nondiseased individuals. It is human nature to seek explanations for tragedies. So it should not surprise us that people who are sick have thought deeply about what caused their problem and may have an overly detailed or even distorted picture of the past. There are many examples that illustrate this point. One occurred in the Armed Forces during the Second World War. Some savants hypothesized that aviators who had crashed their airplanes might have been accident prone as youngsters. If this were true, it would certainly be important to know so these dangerous men might be identified and kept out of the cockpit. A case-control type of study was performed comparing flyers who had crashed their planes with a group of wreckless pilots. Both groups were asked to report any accidents that occurred to them as children. Lo and behold, the flyers with the bad safety records emerged as several times more accident prone than their colleagues. Hypothesis proven! Fortunately wiser heads realized that the trauma of crashing one's airplane might lead to self-indicting ruminations about the past. The experiment was repeated; this time the questions about accidents were asked of flyers as they came into the service, before any crashes had occurred. Freed of the problem of biased recall, investigators found that self-reported accident proneness was not useful for predicting pilots who would have future accidents.

A more recent example comes from a case-control study seeking causes of recurrent urinary-tract infection among young women [1]. Here the cases were women between the ages of 18 and 35 who had experienced at least three documented urinary-tract infections (UTIs). The control group was made up of women of the same age who were healthy attendees of the same student health clinic. A questionnaire was given to these two groups of women asking them to report on a number of their habits, including sexual activities, hygiene, and patterns of voiding. One striking difference that emerged between the groups was that women with recurrent urinary tract infections reported that they often delayed micturation despite feeling an urge to void. This attribute was present for 61 percent of the cases and in only 11 percent of comparison subjects.

The potential for selective recall is considerable. Women who have experienced repeated urinary-tract infections have good reason to have pondered their voiding habits, much more so than unaffected women. The painful urination that frequently accompanies a UTI certainly causes one to focus on the voiding process. Women may become extremely conscious of holding their urine because of the discomfort voiding engenders and report the habit of delayed urination more frequently than women who have not experienced infections, who have little reason to have thought about the problem.

Assessing Recall Bias. Any evidence that the researcher has checked on the memory of subjects should be welcomed and is notice to the reader that authors are on their toes. In a case-control study evaluating estrogen therapy given to women to relieve menopause symptoms and the subsequent risk of developing breast cancer [14], the authors were aware that the history of drug use given by women who had breast cancer might be biased toward the recall of use of estrogens. This was especially likely in view of the substantial controversy the topic has generated in the lay press. The investigators took the additional trouble to review subjects' medical records to document estrogen use as well as check records from major pharmacies in the community. Thus, three estimates of estrogen use were obtained. The researchers were able to show that recall bias did not seem to be playing a role. Estimates of the increased likelihood of breast cancer in high-dosage estrogen users were similar for the three data sources.

Alternate sources of data are not always available. Another way of assessing the possible role of recall bias is to note how cases respond to questions that are not related to the outcome. Some investigators will even include dummy items—questions they feel are unrelated to urinary-tract infections, cancer, or angina—and see if there is a differential response rate between cases and controls. Cases who are exhibiting selective recall should overrespond and identify a large number of items as potentially related to the outcome. So a useful tip for the clinical reader is to take note of how specific the list of associated factors is. If cancer victims recall heavy utilization of five or six different medications, watch out! If only one of a large list of drugs or behaviors has a higher frequency in cases than controls, selective recall is probably less likely. In the recurrent urinary-tract-infection study we have just discussed, the authors report little difference in sexual and hygiene habits between the cases and controls; it is the difference in voiding habits that stands out. If recall bias were occurring, we would expect to see differences between the groups in reporting of other behaviors, such as frequency of sexual activity, as well.

Although not all case-control studies are able to provide evidence that selective recall is not a problem, savvy investigators will at least be cognizant of the importance of this potential bias in their work and report any measures they took to try to master it.

Selection of Controls

The soft underbelly of the case-control study is the selection of appropriate comparison subjects. The idea, of course, is to find a comparison group that looks just like the cases except that the comparison subjects don't have heart disease, bronchitis, or low satisfaction. This creates all sorts of difficulties. It is almost impossible to find a control group that is so obliging. Control subjects who do not have the outcome of interest are likely to share other dissimilarities from subjects who are cases. When investigators announced a possible relationship between coffee consumption and heart attack [9], the appropriateness of their comparison group was challenged [10]. As part of the Boston Collaborative Drug Surveillance Program, Jick et al. had taken drug histories on a large number of hospitalized patients [9]. Records indicated that patients recovering from myocardial infarction (MI) consumed more coffee than did hospitalized patients with other diseases. The interpretation of the data was that coffee drinking is a factor leading to heart attack. Critics countered, however, that using a comparison group of hospitalized patients may have created a false association between coffee consumption and MI [10]. They reasoned that many hospitalized patients have illnesses that are exacerbated by caffeine, such as, peptic-ulcer disease or recurrent cardiac arrhythmias. These patients may have been advised by their physicians to restrict coffee intake. The real test is whether the coffee-drinking habits of people outside the hospital are different from people who experience heart attack.

An inappropriate control group can have the opposite effect and obscure an important link between a disease and its cause. Suppose, for example, that hospitalized lung-cancer patients are questioned regarding smoking habits. If reports of these patients are compared with those of hospital patients who do not have cancer, the connection between smoking and lung cancer may appear spuriously low. Many hospitalized patients may be suffering from other smoking-related diseases, such as, emphysema, bronchitis, or heart disease. They may admit to cigarette usage every bit as high as patients with lung cancer and the strong association between smoking and cancer that would appear if a population of healthy controls were used is lost.

Helping Control-Group Problems

Multiple Controls. One way to deal with the problem of appropriate controls is to utilize more than one comparison group. This way, several estimates of the relationship between the factor under study and the outcome are available. When investigators from the Boston collaborative drug study were evaluating the possible relationship between breast cancer in women and the use of reserpine [3], a commonly prescribed antihypertensive agent, they appreciated the fact that hospitalized control patients might have other diseases that would cause them to use antihypertensive medication, thus underestimating possible effects of reserpine on development of breast cancer. Patients on a medical service who were suffering from cardiovascular diseases, for example, would be particularly likely to have been exposed to antihypertensive drugs. The authors dealt with this problem by eliminating as controls women whose primary reason for hospitalization was a cardiovascular disease. They also selected two entirely different control populations. One group of women came from medical services of the hospitals and the second group from surgical wards. The reasoning was that by using two different estimates of the use of reserpine in non-breast-cancer patients a more accurate result would be achieved. In fact, the authors found very similar rates of reserpine use among both control groups. This rate was substantially lower than that reported by the cancer patients and suggested a link between the use of the drug and the disease (*see* table 3–1).

Community Controls. Many investigators feel that biases are likely with any group of hospitalized patients and prefer including a control group drawn from a general, nonhospitalized population. A paper that attempted to determine environmental and social features that distinguished children seen in a psychiatric outpatient clinic from other children demonstrates why this may be wise [13]. In this study, a sample of children seen in several psychiatric outpatient facilities was contrasted with two control groups. The first was a hospital control group that consisted of children from the pediatric clinic, the ophthalmology clinic, and children who had had an appendectomy or tonsillectomy. The second group was a so-called community control; these children came from the same neighborhood as the cases but were not part of an identified hospital or clinic population. The authors queried parents of the children in each of these three groups about a host of factors ranging from whether the child had nightmares and temper tantrums to the marital relationship of the parents, progress in school, and whether or not the child was spanked. Not surprisingly, children from the psychiatric clinic showed more disruptive behavior and disrupted families than control children. However, a "striking and unexpected finding was

Table 3-1 Antihypertensive Drug (AHD) Use Among Breast-Cancer Patients and Controls

	Reserpine Users	Users of Other AHD	Nonusers of AHD	Total
Breast-cancer cases	11 (7.3%)	7 (4.7%)	132 (88.0%)	150
Surgical controls	13 (2.2%)	29 (4.8%)	558 (93.0%)	600
Medical controls	13 (2.2%)	26 (4.3%)	561 (93.5%)	600

From Boston Collaborative Drug Surveillance Program [3]. Reprinted with permission.

the difference between the hospital control and population control (patients)." Factors such as parental loss, fears, temper tantrums, nightmares, and reports of maladjustment by teachers occurred much more frequently among control children chosen from the clinics than among those taken from the neighborhood. The difference was seen despite the intentional selection of hospital controls who had minor illnesses and surgical procedures. It suggests that children who get into the medical system, regardless of the reason, have characteristics that differ from those of a group of community kids.

Use of community controls put an interesting wrinkle into the reserpine-breast cancer story. The Boston collaborative group was not the only band of investigators to report an association between reserpine and breast cancer. Several other studies were published about the same time that also noted this relationship [2,6]. These studies also utilized hospitalized patients as controls. When subsequent reports utilizing comparison subjects drawn from a community sample came out, the worm turned [11,12]. Mack and coinvestigators showed that while women with breast cancer used somewhat more reserpine than community-control women, they also had higher rates of use of estrogens, barbiturates, and other antihypertensive medication [11]. The authors surmise that this increased use of drugs among women with breast cancer indicates these women are high utilizers of medical care—a trait of socioeconomically advantaged individuals. Since breast cancer is associated with high socioeconomic status, reserpine may simply be a marker for social class rather than a carcinogenic agent.

Matching. One way of dealing with factors that may confuse the comparison between cases and controls is to employ a technique known as matching. This is a term frequently encountered in descriptions of study methods. It means that investigators have made an effort to select control subjects who share particular characteristics with the cases. Matching has a specific purpose. It improves the efficiency of a study by keeping constant or controlling factors that are known to be related to the outcome and may confound or confuse results if they occur disproportionately in the groups that are being compared.

Suppose we wish to evaluate a hunch we have developed that smoking cigars causes people to lose their hair. To study this question in the case-control mode, we first select a group of balding patients from the dermatology clinic—patients who are undergoing a fancy, hair-implantation procedure. As soon as they feel up to wrinkling their brows, we quiz them about their past habits making special note of cigar smoking. We then need to ask the same questions of a comparison group. A little thought suggests that trotting down the hallway to the pediatric clinic would be unwise. The youngsters there, although clinic patients, bear little resemblance to the patients undergoing hair transplants. The obvious difference, age, is an important one because it is related to the habit and the outcome. Cigar smoking is an activity that increases with age; so does baldness. One would expect a higher rate of cigar smoking among the dermatology clinic patients because they are older, not because cigars cause baldness. We would be ill-advised to advertise a link between stogie puffing and alopecia without some way of accounting for the role of age.

Matching reduces competing explanations for the outcome in question. If we select age-matched controls to compare with our bald patients—that is, choose subjects who are close in age to our cases—we would eliminate or control any confusion about whether it is really smoking or just age that is related to hair loss. If we still find higher smoking rates among cases it is not because of differential ages in the groups. This kind of matching may be done on a case-by-case basis where each bald patient is matched with a hairy subject who is within one or two years of being the same age. It may also be accomplished in groups, where both cases and controls are chosen from patients who fall within a specified age range. Age is probably the most commonly matched variable because it is related to so many habits and diseases that come under study. Sex, race, and socioeconomic status are other commonly used variables but matching may be carried out on any factor from apple-cider drinking to exposure to zinc smelters. It is a lovely technique for creating order in the world. However, there is a price to be paid for matching.

Wasted Matching. You can match subjects on as many different characteristics as you wish. In our bald example, we could select for the comparison group only controls who were of the same age, race, sex, socioeconomic status, religious persuasion, eye color, and political party as the cases. That would eliminate all those factors as competing explanations for hair loss. Our study might be a long time in completion, however. If every comparison subject must meet seven or eight matching criteria the field of eligible patients dwindles considerably. Tremendous time and effort will be required to find subjects who fulfill the list of demands. We will have made life unnecessarily difficult on ourselves, not only by choosing a great number of items, but by selecting as matching factors several characteristics that have no relationship or association with baldness. Age and sex are important. We know that older people are more liable to hair loss and that men are more susceptible than women. With old men comprising the bulk of cigar smokers, matching can help; but the color of someone's eyes bears little relationship to either the propensity to baldness or the use of cigars.

Overmatching. There is a second, more-substantial cost of matching. An investigator can overmatch. Since matching equalizes the occurrence of a factor in the groups that are being compared, once cases and controls are matched by age, sex, or whatever, these factors can no longer be evaluated as possible etiological agents. As an obvious example, suppose we are fledgling hematologists, unencumbered by previous knowledge about factors that cause anemia. We have discovered a group of patients with severe anemia who have unusual, sickle-shaped red cells in their blood smears. In an attempt to learn more about the etiology of this disease, we devise a clever case-control, observational study in which we match patients who have the anemia with nonanemic medical patients of the same age, race, and sex. We note in passing that the cases all happen to be black and, therefore, we select only blacks as control patients. We have overmatched. By matching for race we have lost our ability to show that sickle-cell anemia has a genetic basis as reflected by differential occurrence in whites and blacks.

There are two rules for matching that readers should tuck under their critical belts:

1. Matching is only useful if factors that are matched are known to be related to both the outcome and to other characteristics under study.

2. Matching a factor eliminates it as a possible explanation of the outcome.

In Brief. The reader should ask the following when considering choice of the comparison group.

1. What sort of population do the control subjects represent? Do they behave like people in the general population or like people who have filtered through the health-care system?

2. Are there likely to be relationships between the control population and the factors under study that would influence the results?

3. Was matching used appropriately?

A good medical study should give complete details on the methods used for selecting comparison subjects and describe the attributes of these controls. More elegant studies will use several control groups in an effort to put results into perspective.

Selection of Cases

The way in which cases are selected for study is also of interest. Disease states are seldom homogeneous, and the forces that propel any group of patients to a particular research setting may create a very unusual sample of subjects. Patients who form the cases in a tertiary referral center, for example, may have characteristics quite unlike those seen in a family-medicine practice. Women referred to a medical center for recurrent urinary-tract infections may respond to a questionnaire about their voiding habits and sexual activities very differently from patients at a university health service. One could imagine that referred women have already been screened for predisposing factors like delayed voiding and represent cases with an unusually large proportion of structural abnormalities of the urinary tract. The cause of recurrent infections for these cases would be quite different from that for university health service patients.

Another consideration when scrutinizing cases is how well defined the disease is. Is the author talking about a carefully delineated, homogeneous problem? The breadth and specificity of an outcome are important to assigning possible causative agents. For example, despite the layperson's view that someday science will unravel the mysteries of the cause of cancer, most medical people understand that many diseases fit under the general rubric of cancer and have a variety of etiologies. No one would consider doing a case-control study mixing cases of leukemia, Wilm's tumor, osteogenic sarcoma, and tumors of the bowel. Even within a specific tumor site we know that etiologies may be different depending upon the histologic type of cancer. Asking patients with adenocarcinoma of the lung about their past cigarette consumption will give different results from the same question applied to a group of patients with squamous cell cancer. The strong association between lung cancer and smoking only holds for the latter type of tumor.

Who cases are, where they come from, and what spectrum of disease they represent is important information. We will return to consider issues of subject selection again as we look at cross-sectional, follow-up and experimental designs.

Other Biases

We have discussed selective recall as a case-control-design bias. Other potential biases afflict the methodology. Bias can occur any time groups being compared differ systematically in a way that is related to the outcome. Study results may be upset when we fail to recognize important inequalities of information gathering, reporting, sampling, utilization, or observation between groups. Bias leads us to believe that we have found an important increase in the rate of childhood accidents in flyers who crash their planes when in fact we are measuring the heightened recall of traumatized individuals. Any time a reader suspects that a group under study goes to doctors more, has more complete records kept, is watched more closely, questioned more thoroughly, subjected to more tests, or represents an unusual subgroup of a population, the possibility of bias exists. Patients who are on potentially hazardous drugs like steroids or estrogens are likely to be observed closely for the occurrence of gastric ulcers or uterine cancer, so these diseases are found at early presymptomatic stages that might go undetected in patients not on red-flag medication. Similarly, patients with diseases that have known risk factors or causes, such as, emphysema or bladder cancer, may be questioned in greater detail about use of tobacco or artificial sweeteners than control subjects. A voluntary response bias can arise when cases who think they have been exposed to a potential carcinogen like arsenic or asbestos return mailed questionnaires at a higher rate than controls. Sackett has listed 35 variations on the bias theme [15]. The names and nuances are of less importance to clinicians than an understanding of the basic concept.

Readers should not only look for biases, but assess the author's ability to identify and deal with these problems of equivalency. In a study that sought predictive factors in the social environment of patients with Hodgkin's disease [5], the authors went to elegant lengths to demonstrate that information obtained from noncancer controls was similar to that given by Hodgkin's cases. Interviewers were asked not only to rate the reliability of interviews but to record the amount of time spent talking to each subject. The investigators are then able to report that information biases do not appear to be responsible for differences found since not only was subject reliability found to be similar for cases and controls, but time spent in the interviews was almost identical, averaging 28.1 minutes and 26.7 minutes for the two groups, respectively.

Summary

Once a study has been identified as a case-control design, ask the following:

1. How dependable is the information obtained from the past? Are data available from written sources such as medical records, and are these data likely to have been collected in a reliable manner?

2. If data are based on recollection of subjects, is recall bias operating? What attempts have authors made to assess the effect of this potential bias?

3. How like the cases are control subjects? Are they really from a similar population, differing only in the absence of disease? Or are

there other differences that might bear a relationship to the outcome under study and create a spurious appearance of relationship between the characteristic under study and the outcome? Have techniques such as matching been employed in an attempt to control these confounding or confusing relationships?

4. What kind of a population do the cases represent? Are they a heterogeneous representation of the disease or outcome in question or a highly selected population for whom responses have limited generalizability?

5. Are other biases evident? Do we know more about cases because they have been under closer surveillance, volunteered more information, or been subjected to more extensive testing than control subjects?

Passing this critical barrage is a difficult task for a case-control study, but the methods used to conduct studies of this sort are continually improving. A critical look at studies for these common limitations of design may lead to the disquieting conclusion that a number of efforts are not credible. On the other hand, we should feel some joy that investigators are becoming increasingly facile with this challenging methodology and often succeed in providing useful information with maximum efficiency.

References

1. ADATTO, K., DOEBELE, K. G., GALLAND, L., AND GRANOWETTER, L. Behavioral factors and urinary tract infection. *JAMA* 241:2525–2526, 1979.

2. ARMSTRONG, B., STEVENS, N., AND DOLL, R. Retrospective study of the association between use of rauwolfia derivatives and breast cancer in English women. *Lancet* 2:672–675, 1974.

3. BOSTON COLLABORATIVE DRUG SURVEILLANCE PROGRAM. Reserpine and breast cancer. *Lancet* 2:669–671, 1974.

4. COLE, P. The evolving case-control study. *J. Chron. Dis.* 32:15–27, 1979.

5. GUTENSOHN, N. AND COLE, P. Childhood social environment and Hodgkin's disease. *N. Engl. J. Med.* 304:135–140, 1981.

6. HEINONEN, O. P., SHAPIRO, S., TUONIMEN, L., AND TURUNEN, M. I. Reserpine use in relation to breast cancer. *Lancet* 2:675–677, 1974.

7. HERBST, A. L. AND SCULLY, R. E. Adenocarcinoma of the vagina in adolescence: A report of 7 cases including 6 clear-cell carcinomas (so-called mesonephromas). *Cancer* 25:745–757, 1970.

8. HERBST, A. L., ULFELDER, H., AND POSKANZER, D. C. Adenocarcinoma of the vagina: Association of maternal stilbestrol therapy with tumor appearance in young women. *N. Engl. J. Med.* 284:878–881, 1971.

9. JICK, H., MIETTINEN, O. S., NEFF, R. K., SHAPIRO, S., HEINONEN, O. P., AND SLONE, D. Coffee and myocardial infarction. *N. Engl. J. Med.* 289:63–67, 1973.

10. KANNEL, W. B. AND DAWBER, T. R. Coffee and coronary disease. *N. Engl. J. Med.* 289:101, 1973.

11. MACK, T. M., HENDERSON, B. E., GERKINS, V. R., ARTHUR, M., BAPTISTA, J., AND PIKE, M. C. Reserpine and breast cancer in a retirement community. *N. Engl. J. Med.* 292:1366–1371, 1975.

12. O'FALLON, W. M., LABARTHE, D. R., AND KURLAND, L. T. Rauwolfia derivatives and breast cancer. A case-control study in Olmstead County, Minnesota. *Lancet* 2:292–296, 1975.

13. OLEINICK, M. S., BAHN, A. K., EISENBERG, L., AND LILIENFELD, A. M. Early socialization experiences and intrafamilial environment: A study of psychiatric outpatient and control group children. *Arch. Gen. Psychiat.* 15:344–353, 1966.

14. ROSS, R. K., PAGANINI-HILL, A., GERKINS, V. R., ET AL. A case-control study of menopausal estrogen therapy and breast cancer. *JAMA* 243:1635–1639, 1980.

15. SACKETT, D. L. Bias in analytic research. *J. Chron. Dis.* 32:51–63, 1979.

FOUR

Study Design: The Cross-Sectional and Follow-Up Approach

Had we but world enough and time,
this cohort study were no crime.
—adapted from Andrew Marvell

After discussing observational studies that start with subjects who already have an outcome or disease, we will turn in this chapter to evaluating designs that utilize the cross-sectional and follow-up approaches. As outlined in chapter 2, these studies tackle the task of providing explanations by assembling groups of subjects that represent either a general, nondiseased population or people who share features we think might predispose them to a particular outcome. Subjects are classified by characteristics such as high cholesterol, crowded living conditions, or occupational exposure to benzene. Then they are either simultaneously sorted by diseases they already have (for example, heart disease, mental illness, or leukemia) or followed for a period of time to see what develops.

In the cross-sectional or prevalence approach it is all done at once, in a single slice of time. Second-grade schoolgirls are screened to see how many have asymptomatic bacteriuria; men over 65 years of age are given rectal examinations to determine the frequency of prostatic hypertrophy; cottonmill workers are classified according to dust exposure and given pulmonary function tests to find those with evidence of brown-lung disease. These are typical examples of the cross-sectional or prevalence type of design schematized in figure 4–1. Often subjects identified in these cross-sectional efforts go on to become the cohort or population of interest for a follow-up study. The girls with bacteriuria are observed for ten years to see who develops renal complications, the old men with prostatic enlargement are watched to see who gets obstructive symptoms; workers with pulmonary impairment are further classified according to smoking habits and followed for progression of disease. Figure 4–2 recalls this approach. In this chapter, we will take a closer look at the contributions these study designs can make and learn some critical questions to ask each time one of the strategies is encountered.

Cross-Sectional Designs

From the quick glance at cross-sectional designs offered in chapter 2, one might infer that the approach is a country cousin to the more elegant follow-up design. It is true that prevalence studies are often conducted as screening and classification preambles to larger, follow-up efforts. Before the incidence of heart disease in a community is studied, the population must be evaluated for current cardiac status and sorted by characteristics such as blood pressure, smoking, and cholesterol. However, in an increasing number of studies, the cross-sectional design is serving as the appetizer, main course, and dessert. In reviewing the designs utilized in articles from three of the most influential clinical journals, the Fletchers note that cross-sectional studies have become increasingly prevalent (pun intended) [6]. In 1946, 24 percent of 151 journal articles surveyed were classified as cross-sectional in design compared with 44 percent of articles published in 1976. This increasing popularity indicates the design has considerable flexibility and applicability beyond providing initial classification of patients for subsequent follow-up endeavors. Some of these applications are noted in table 4–1.

The cross-sectional strategy shares some advantages of the case-control design. It is strong on efficiency. Conclusions are based on information collected at the same time so investigators are not obliged to wait months or years in the anticipation of an outcome. Everything is done on the spot, often from information that is already at hand. Pharmacy records of antibiotics ordered in a community

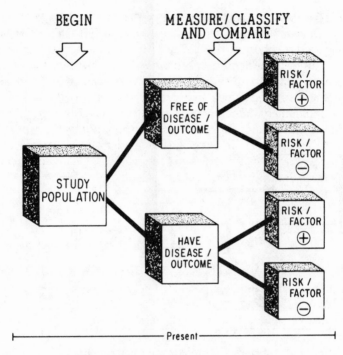

Figure 4-1. *Cross-sectional study design.*

hospital are searched and usage is detailed according to medical specialty. Patients with juvenile rheumatoid arthritis are tested for histocompatibility antigens and compared by age and symptom patterns. However, while cross-sectional designs enjoy economies of time and trouble, they fall prey to some difficulties. Several of these can be particularly bothersome. Two that we will mull over in some detail are patient selection and antecedent-consequent relationships.

Selection

Population Selection. The kinds of subjects that find their way into cross-sectional studies can have a major influence on results. Earlier we discussed generalizability as an issue that must be addressed in reviewing studies. It is important to know if the acne patients described as responding favorably to topical treatment with

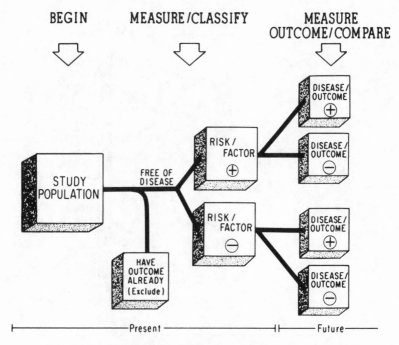

Figure 4-2. Follow-up study design.

clindamycin are enough like patients we see that comparable therapeutic results may be expected, or that our patients on birth control pills share features with patients an article describes as being at increased risk for pulmonary embolism. Sometimes a study offers a view of health risks or outcomes that is accurate for a very special group of patients but that lacks relevance for the practice of the typical clinician. A mismatch is particularly likely when the study population is drawn from a tertiary hospital or referral center. These patients often pass through a complex filter before reaching the meccas. About 20 years ago, White et al. created a model depicting the selection process that takes place before patients arrive at tertiary medical centers [13]. As figure 4–3 suggests, only a fraction of potential patients in a community become subjects for study in a referral center. Those that do are unlikely to be representative of the 999 folks back home. Information gathered on such highly selected patients can be misleading.

Table 4-1 Some Uses of the Cross-Sectional Approach

Use	Example
Evaluate a new test or the new application of an old one	HLA-B27 antigen to characterize subsets of juvenile rheumatoid arthritis
	C-reactive protein to predict invasive streptococcal disease
Evaluate the predictive capability of clinical features	Relationship of fever and age to bacteremia
	Accuracy of the rectal examination in diagnosing prostate carcinoma
Identify etiological agents or causative factors	*Salmonella*-induced diarrhea at the church barbecue supper
	Lactose intolerance as cause of recurrent abdominal pain
Determine the prevalence of a problem	Drug use in a high-school population
	Disabilities among the elderly related to age and economic status

An example of population selection at work may be seen from comparing two studies on the etiology of low back pain. One of these reports comes from the Mayo Clinic [7], a very special referral center, the other from a family-practice setting [12]. Investigators from each of these sites reviewed the cases of low back pain they had seen over a period of time and described the frequency with which herniated intervertebral disc disease was diagnosed. According to the Mayo Clinic, suspected discs are responsible for 22 percent of cases of low back pain; in the family medicine practice only 4.4 percent of low back pain sufferers were suspected of having disc problems, with only two of 140 cases reviewed (1.4 percent) actually confirmed by myelogram and surgically treated. The most likely factor contributing to the varying results is the dissimilarity in the study populations. Most patients who go to Mayo have been to at least one other doctor. Many less-important back problems never get referred, so by the time patients reach the clinic, a higher proportion of the pool has

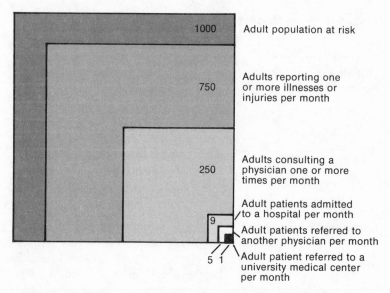

Figure 4-3. Monthly prevalence estimates of illness in the community and the roles of physicians, hospitals, and university medical centers in the provision of medical care (adults 16 years of age and over). (From White, K. L. et al. [13] by permission of the New England Journal of Medicine 265:890, 1961.)

more severe disease, such as herniated discs. The general practice takes on all comers and sees a greater percentage of less-complicated problems. Their experience more accurately reflects the frequency of disc disease in a general population than does the Mayo report.

Subject Selection. Once an author has chosen a population, it is important to find out who within that group becomes a study subject. There are a variety of ways authors can select samples. They may attempt to enroll every eligible subject in the study. That is fine for small populations, but with larger groups, it is not feasible. One approach to dealing with bigger populations is systematic sampling, which involves selecting every second or third, etc. patient who is available or picking only patients with even numbers as the last digit of their medical records. Another technique is random sampling in which a portion of available patients is chosen by selection of random numbers or drawing from a hat. This assures each member of the population an equal chance of being included in the study. The question readers must ask is whether the sampling technique employed guards against the selection of a biased or unrepresentative sample. Authors may report that patients were selected at random when, in fact, strict randomizing techniques, such as using a random-numbers table or other unbiased procedures, were not used. Used colloquially, random selection means unplanned or haphazard sampling. It suggests authors had no sampling plan in mind but simply took a convenience sample of subjects to enroll in the study. This is not good enough. Very unrepresentative samples of subjects can be obtained when laissez-faire sampling techniques are used.

Let us return for a look at the study on outpatient blood cultures as an aid to diagnosing the cause of fever in children [10]. This is a good example of a cross-sectional design that seeks evidence for the utility of the new application of a test (blood cultures) to clarify a clinical problem (fever of unknown origin). All febrile children attending the walk-in clinic during a three-month period were eligible for study. Blood cultures were obtained from these children to ascertain the prevalence of bacteremia, and subjects were simultaneously cross-classified by characteristics such as degree of fever, age, and white blood count to augment the clinician's predictive power (*see* table 4–2).

We have seen in chapter 1 that the message of this study becomes clouded in the absence of detailed clinical information about the subjects. It should, nonetheless, provide a reasonable estimate of the frequency with which bacteremia occurs. Unfortunately, haphazard sampling adds even more fog to the scene. The authors do well in clearly defining fever as a "rectal temperature of 38.3°C or higher or an oral temperature of 37.8°C or higher" but report as their sampling technique only that "physicians of the pediatric service were requested to obtain a blood culture from febrile patients." It turns out that during the three-month study period 2,059 children visited the clinic who met the fever criteria. Of these, only 415, or 20 percent, actually had blood cultures obtained. In other words, only one-fifth of eligible patients were included. With no more information than we have at hand regarding the sampling procedure, can we assume that children included represent the entire population in an unbiased fashion? Probably not. Children who are cultured are likely to be kids who worried physicians because they appeared to be

Table 4–2   Factors Associated with Bacteremia in Febrile Children

Factor	Percent of Patients with Positive Blood Cultures
Fever	
less than 38.9	0.9
38.9 to 39.9	6.6
40.0 or greater	8.0
Age	
less than 12 mos.	6.7
13 to 24 mos.	4.6
25 mos. or greater	2.7
White-Blood-Cell Count	
less than 10,000	1.1
10,000 to 19,900	6.1
20,000 or greater	11.6

Based on McGowan, J. E., Jr., et al. [10] by permission of the *New England Journal of Medicine*, 288:1310, 1973.

toxic, that is, children who were suspected of having bacterial infection such as pneumonia or meningitis. Youngsters who appeared to have benign febrile illnesses, such as roseola, or viral gastroenteritis would be less-promising candidates for culture. Any estimate of the frequency of bacteremia in this selected sample is probably an overestimate of the likelihood of positive blood cultures among the general population of febrile children. The results may give us an idea of how often bacteria can be isolated from the blood of sicker youngsters, but without a clear description of the selection that went on, we have no way of generalizing the data. Had the authors provided us with comparative information about the clinical condition of patients sampled and those excluded, the data they provide might be more useful.

Antecedent-Consequent Relationships

Cross-sectional studies fall prey to a chicken and egg dilemma. Since information related to a subject's outcome is collected at the same time as data on the possible causative or predictive factor, it is not always clear which comes first. Does the attribute or characteristic really lead to the effect or disease, or does the outcome in some way predispose people to acquire factors or characteristics that appear to be predictive? An example comes from the literature on childhood lead poisoning. Recall from chapter 3 that, while severe lead intoxication is known to cause seizures and encephalopathy, the effect of lower levels of chronic lead exposure on neurologic development has been an important research question. Investigators from New York hypothesized that lead intoxication might be an important cause of hyperactivity among children [4]. To test their idea, they assembled several samples of children from a pediatric outpatient clinic. Some of these children carried the diagnosis of hyperactivity, some had been diagnosed and treated as having lead poisoning, and some were nonhyperactive comparisons. The strategy was simply to measure blood and urine lead levels among these children to see if differences could be found between the groups. The investigators found that for children identified as being hyperactive "without a presumed cause," lead levels were substantially higher than for the nonhyperactive controls. They conclude that these increased lead levels make it "conceivable that one consequence of this constant minimal poisonous assault is hyperactivity." However, there is an important reservation one must raise about this interpretation. As the authors themselves query, "might the lead levels recorded be a consequence of the child's hyperactivity rather than a hyperactivity cause?" It is a good question. Lead poisoning may indeed cause hyperactive behavior. However, it is also known that hyperactive children tend to have high rates of other untoward behaviors, such as pica, the ingestion of nonfood substances. Children who have hyperactivity may eat more lead paint than the comparison group, so the evidence of lead accumulation in the body becomes a reflection of the hyperactive behavior rather than a cause of it.

Another example are reports from cross-sectional studies that explore childhood obesity. A common finding has been that children who are overweight are less active than their normal-weight contemporaries. The conclusion drawn from these reports is that children who have low levels of activity are more likely to become obese, but again, antecedent-consequent relationships are muddied when data on causes and effects are collected at the same time. It is also plausible that children with weight problems have difficulty getting around and are inactive because of their obesity rather than fat because they are inactive.

The antecedent-consequent problem is a frailty cross-sectional designs share with case-control efforts. The case-control study that looked at characteristics of women who suffer recurrent urinary-tract infections offers another example of potentially confusing cause and effect [1]. In that study, women with recurrent urinary infections reported the habit of delayed micturation. This delayed voiding was presumed to be responsible for the infections. However, it is possible that the painful urination that accompanied the bladder infections in fact promoted the habit of delayed voiding. Infection causes the habit; the habit does not cause infection. While this makes a nice illustration, it also can be argued that most women with urinary-tract infections experience frequency as well as pain and find withholding difficult. It is probably more an academic exercise than a clinical reality to suggest that the disease creates the characteristic in this particular situation.

Follow-Up Studies

The follow-up or cohort design is generally considered to be the crème de la crème of observational methodologies. It is unencumbered by many of the problems that beset the case-control and cross-sectional approaches. Since data are gathered prospectively rather than from rooting through records of the past, they may be collected in a comprehensive and uniform fashion. No need to worry whether height and weight were recorded in the chart or whether blood pressure was accurately measured. Investigators can set up the rules before they begin. Nor is recall bias a problem since patients are not being asked to recall events of the past but will be followed into the future to see which outcomes develop. Antecedent and consequence relationships are also made clear as patients are classified by characteristics before the disease or outcome becomes manifest. Voiding habits of women would be ascertained before anyone develops a urinary-tract infection; activity levels of children of normal weight can be documented before they are followed to see who develops obesity. It is all much tidier, there is much more control over the quality of the data, and there is greater clarity in the sequence of events. Had we, as Andrew Marvell suggests, no constraints of resources and unlimited time it would be the ideal strategy. Unfortunately, substantial costs are likely to be incurred in following large populations and "Time's winged chariot" does, in fact, press us.

Follow-up studies are also not without their methodologic weak points. In addition to that plague of observational studies, population selection, there are three other afflictions that we have not examined thus far: loss to follow-up, changes in subject characteristics, and surveillance bias.

Selection

Follow-up designs are susceptible to selection problems. An elegant illustration comes from the literature on febrile convulsions in children. In a typical case a toddler of one to two years of age will be bundled to the emergency room by frantic parents. The child seemed fine, they report, until he suddenly fell to the floor, eyes rolled back, in a generalized tonic-clonic convulsion. The seizure lasted for only a few minutes and not until the aftermath did the parents realize the child was febrile to 104°. This is a horrifying experience for parents. When the initial anxiety abates, their most immediate concerns are, "Will it happen again?" and "Does this mean my child has epilepsy?" Good questions! Just the kind requiring a good natural history or follow-up study to answer. The answer, however, is very much dependent on the kind of population whose natural history is assessed. A study from Edinburgh, for example, followed 200 children admitted to a teaching hospital with the diagnosis of febrile convulsion [12]. They found that almost 17 percent of these children had subsequent nonfebrile recurrences, which is a fairly large number. However, if the response to parents about epilepsy is based on a Greek study [8], febrile seizure patients will have a 65 percent chance of having later nonfebrile seizures. For those that find this prospect much too distressing, Nelson and Ellenberg give an overall risk of nonfebrile recurrences of only 3 percent [11]. That's certainly more encouraging! With such a wide variety of results, all coming from reputable journals, how do we know whom to believe?

In fact, all these studies may be right. They may all accurately portray the risk of recurrent seizures for the particular population they are observing. Readers must decide how the groups of patients reported compare with those they will be seeing. In this particular situation, the Scottish study reports on children who were hospitalized at a large medical center, the Greek study describes patients referred to a special developmental evaluation center, and Nelson's patients come from a cohort of 15,000 newborn infants from 11 U.S. cities who were followed for some years to detect neurologic abnormalities. Ethnic differences notwithstanding, the broad population sample best reflects the kind of patients most doctors encounter and suggests that for most children who experience febrile convulsions the risk of subsequent, nonfebrile attacks is small.

To confirm their impression that sample selection plays an important role in the results one finds, Ellenberg and Nelson made some further comparisons [5]. They reviewed 26 published articles that estimated the likelihood of nonfebrile seizures for children with febrile fits and classified findings by two categories of study populations. One group contained clinic-based studies—those that followed patients who came from hospital clinics or specialty referral units. The other group contained population-based studies—where a clearly defined general population was used. The comparative rates of recurrences are depicted in figure 4–4. Estimates for clinic-based studies are highly variable, ranging up to 75 percent; figures derived from population-based studies are much lower and remarkably consistent at about 3 percent.

Every study will have its own population of subjects, and each will have limits of generalizability. Readers must decide how closely subjects described in the study mirror patients they will be treating. Good authors will help in this task. Readers have a right to expect a reasonable amount of information about patients described in any study. What are their demographic characteristics? Where do they come from? Have they been referred from other medical-care facilities or come on their own? What is the reputation of the facility where the patients were gathered? Is it known to attract certain kinds of patients with certain kinds of illnesses? Is it a specialty clinic? Only armed with this information can the problem of external validity or generalizability be addressed. If our patients are very unlike those being described in the study, we may be justified in feeling some reluctance to embrace the author's conclusions.

Loss to Follow-Up

No matter how carefully one's sample is chosen, no matter how elegantly representative of the population, if subjects are lost to follow-up we are in trouble. The biggest single problem of follow-

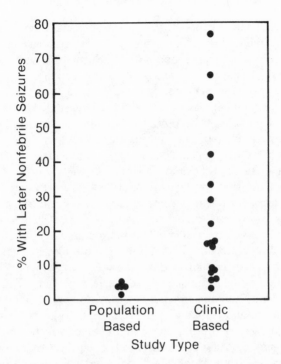

Figure 4-4. *Percentage of children who experienced nonfebrile seizures after one or more febrile seizures, in population-based (left) and clinic-based (right) studies. From Ellenberg, J. H. and Nelson, K. B. [5] by permission of JAMA 243:1338, 1980. Copyright © 1980, American Medical Association.*

up-design investigations is the loss of valuable information through attrition. Subjects change addresses, fail to respond to questionnaires, decide they no longer wish to participate, or just plain cannot be located. Dropouts are unfortunate, not simply because they reduce the numbers of subjects observed, but because the reasons they become lost to follow-up may be related to the outcomes under study. That adds another source of bias.

An illustration comes from the report of a study on the likelihood that women who lose babies will become depressed during the six-month postpartum period [3]. Study subjects included women who had had a stillborn infant or whose babies died in the first seven days of life. A complete sample of mothers who lost babies was taken for one year in an entire English county. For each of these, a comparison subject was chosen from all the mothers residing in the same locale who had had live births in that year. The authors matched the cases and controls by place and time of delivery. It is worth recalling here that while the authors speak of these comparison mothers as controls and refer to perinatal death subjects as cases, they are not utilizing a case-control design. The action of the study is forward and perinatal death is not the outcome but a potential risk factor for postpartum depression. The authors are forced to sample from the total pool of comparison patients, since to have included all live births would have created an extremely large cohort.

Questionnaires were given out at two days, six weeks, and six months postpartum, asking women to report on symptoms related to depression. When returned questionnaires were tallied and evaluated for the presence of depressive symptomatology, a rather surprising finding emerged. "At 6 months, postpartum depression was just as common in women aged under 24 whose babies had survived as in women of the same age whose babies had died." This revelation is certainly contrary to what one would expect. Unfortunately, diligent as the authors were in their attempts to keep track of the women they enrolled in the study, not everyone responded to the questionnaire. And there is reason to believe this loss to follow-up was biased. The authors note that "compared with the control group, fewer of the women whose babies had died responded to the six-month questionnaire." It also happens that in both groups the non-response rate was "more than twice as high" for women whose day two depression scores were high than for those whose rating indicated no depression. This information has some sticky implications. If women failed to respond to questionnaires because they were depressed, the unexpected low rate of postpartum depression among women who lost babies is an artifact of biased follow-up. These women are depressed—so depressed they are not up to completing and returning a depression inventory.

Subject loss is the bane of the follow-up study. A questionnaire is sent to patients asking them to report their satisfaction with a recent visit to the clinic. Only 50 percent respond. Are those who do not respond failing to do so because they are angry and dissatisfied or because they are pleased with the service and have no complaints? A study is designed to follow respiratory function of workers who have occupational exposure to cotton dust. A substantial number of workers cannot be located ten years later when it is time to evaluate their pulmonary status. Is there anything special about the group that cannot be found? Have they all changed jobs because of respiratory incapacity? Have they moved to Arizona so they can breathe? The possibility that attrition in studies is due to the factors being explored is substantial.

There are several ways that investigators can deal with the follow-up problem. Canny readers should check behind the author to see if this homework has been performed.

1. Has the investigator made every effort to track down lost subjects? Repeat mailings, telephone contacts, or home visits give evidence that investigators have been diligent in their efforts to locate wayward subjects and suggest concern about attrition. The authors of the perinatal death and depression report get positive marks for their effort [3]. Second mailings were sent to all nonresponders to the first letter, and health visitors were sent to homes of those who failed to respond to the second mailing. Losses still occurred.

2. Do authors report the rate of follow-up loss and explore the possibility of biased attrition? Recognizing that some loss is inevitable, authors should detail the extent of the problem and offer information on characteristics of the nonrespondents. Authors should be able to provide demographic features, such as, age, sex, and some initial classifying information like responses to the first depression scale. The more information that indicates that the lost sheep are similar to those in the fold, the more comfortable we may feel that an important attrition bias is not influencing results. Any follow-up study that fails to offer information on losses should be viewed with skepticism.

3. Another technique for characterizing nonrespondents or dropouts is to spend some additional effort to contact a representative sample of this total group. This may be a difficult task since initial efforts at contact have been unsuccessful, but the effort expended in attacking a small sample may reward the investigator with important information about the characteristics of these lost subjects.

Change in Habits

Although the follow-up design appears to avoid the messy business of relying on the memories of subjects to catalog habits and exposures of the past, other snares await the best laid of plans. Subjects can change their habits. Smokers quit smoking, the inactive take up jogging, and dieters stop using saccharine. When investigators rely on initial categorizations of smoking activity and use of artificial sweeteners, they may find themselves misclassifying subjects. People thought to be at high risk may alter their lifestyle or reduce their exposure to a drug or environmental contaminant. Those who are thought to be at low risk may begin snacking on potato chips or start work in an asbestos factory. If only small numbers of subjects change their roles in an unselected way, there is not much problem; if many people switch, it can be trouble. In the time it takes to follow the natural history of a group of people, many uncontrolled outside events can occur. A community-health-education campaign may induce subjects to stop smoking or a national fad such as jogging may overtake even the most sedentary of the citizenry. Patients may read in the newspaper about the dangerous side effects of a drug they have been taking and decide to discontinue the medication. There is not a great deal investigators can do to control this phenomenon, but they can periodically reexamine subjects and update classifications. Readers should look for evidence that authors are alert to the issue and reexamine their cohort to see whether habits or exposures have changed.

Surveillance Bias

Another bias in follow-up studies can occur if there is unequal surveillance of subjects being compared. This problem is shared by all the observational designs and occurs any time one group of subjects get scrutinized or examined more closely than others. A case in point is a follow-up study that describes antecedents of child abuse and neglect among premature infants [9]. Investigators collected extensive information on 255 families who had infants admitted to the newborn intensive-care unit of a university medical center. A "psychosocial risk inventory" was created to help identify children who might be subsequent victims of child abuse. Included in the inventory was information such as adequacy of child spacing, social isolation, major life stress, adequacy of child-care arrangements, and financial status. Each family was scored and categorized as being at high or low psychosocial risk. The authors found that after a follow-up period of 6 to 19 months, 10 of 41 infants (24 percent) assigned to the high-risk group were reported to be abused or neglected compared with none of the infants categorized as low psychosocial risk.

That is an impressive difference and suggests the psychosocial scoring system has great utility. Unfortunately a misstep in design opens the way for significant surveillance bias. Infants who were classified as high risk on the basis of their inventory scores were identified to social-service agencies at the time of discharge from the hospital. While this may have been desirable practice from the view-point of supporting families in need of help, it seriously interferes with the ability to give an unbiased assessment of the value of the scoring system. Identifying the infants as high risk for abuse also puts them at high risk of close surveillance and at high risk for being reported for abuse and neglect. It is like examining one group of histologic speci-mens under low-power scan and another group under oil immersion. The closer you look, the more you find. Reading that evidence of neglect included "leaving infants unattended at home, failing to comply with routine immunizations, and failing to provide adequate nutrition" suggests that differential surveillance is contributing to the findings. Low-risk kids are probably also being left unattended; it is just that nobody's watching.

Summary

Having come across a study design you identify as being a cross-sectional or follow-up approach consider the following:

1. How is the study population selected? Do subjects come from a referral center, a general medical practice, or the community at large? Are there special features or characteristics of patients that would select them for membership in this particular population? Are they older, sicker, richer, or do they have more severe manifestations of a given disease? Have they already come through selective filters in the medical system? Do the authors provide sufficient information for you to identify the population and judge its similarity to your own?

2. Are procedures for sampling within this population clearly defined? Can you tell exactly how individual subjects were picked? Were they chosen in a manner that avoids selection bias? Do authors provide evidence that subjects who are eligible but not included in the study are similar to those that have been selected? Do authors acknowledge the potential for selection bias and give evidence of

safeguards used to avoid it or demonstrate that the problem has not affected results?

3. When a cross-sectional approach is utilized, are antecedent-consequent relationships clear? If subjects are simultaneously classified by behaviors or potentially causative characteristics and the effects or outcomes, is cause and effect implied when the sequence of events is not clear? Is it likely the characteristic really leads to the outcome or could people who have certain diseases secondarily acquire characteristics that appear causative?

4. If a follow-up design is utilized, is there loss to follow-up? Are authors careful to detail the methods used to follow subjects and provide information about subjects who stay? Are these nonrespondents or dropouts likely to bias results? Are reasons for attrition likely to be related to outcomes under study? Did subjects fail to answer because they were depressed or leave town because they could not breathe?

5. Did subjects change habits or exposures during the course of study? Have those believed to be at high risk initially changed their status by altering lifestyle, occupation or drug intake? Do authors periodically reexamine their cohorts to see if habits have changed?

6. Is surveillance bias occurring? Are the groups being compared being observed with equal intensity? Or is high-powered scrutiny being applied to certain subjects, which may bias results?

References

1. ADATTO, K., DOEBELE, K. G., GALLAND, L., AND GRANOWETTER, L. Behavioral factors and urinary tract infection. *JAMA* 241:2525–2526, 1979.

2. BARTON, J. E., HAIGHT, R. O., MARSLAND, D. W., AND TEMPLE, T. E., JR. Low back pain in the primary care setting. *J. Fam. Pract.* 3:363–366, 1976.

3. CLARKE, M. AND WILLIAMS, A. J. Depression in women after perinatal death. *Lancet* 1:916–917, 1979.

4. DAVID, O., CLARK, J., AND VOELLER, K. Lead and hyperactivity. *Lancet* 2:900–903, 1972.

5. ELLENBERG, J. H. AND NELSON, K. B. Sample selection and the

natural history of disease: Studies of febrile seizures. *JAMA* 243:1337-1340, 1980.

6. FLETCHER, R. H. AND FLETCHER, S. W. Clinical research in general medical journals: A 30-year perspective. *N. Engl. J. Med.* 301:180-183, 1979.

7. GHORMLEY, R. K. An etiology study of backache and sciatic pain. *Proceedings of the Staff Meetings of the Mayo Clinic* 26:457-463, 1951.

8. GREGORIADES, A. D. A medical and social survey of 231 children with seizures. *Epilepsia* 13:13-20, 1972.

9. HUNTER, R. S., KILSTROM, N., KRAYBILL, E. N., AND LODA, F. Antecedents of child abuse and neglect in premature infants: A prospective study in a newborn intensive care unit. *Pediatrics* 61:629-635, 1978.

10. MCGOWAN, J. E., JR., BRATTON, L., KLEIN, J. O., AND FINLAND, M. Bacteremia in febrile children seen in a "walk-in" pediatric clinic. *N. Engl. J. Med.* 288:1309-1312, 1973.

11. NELSON, K. B. AND ELLENBERG, J. H. Predictors of epilepsy in children who have experienced febrile seizures. *N. Engl. J. Med.* 295:1029-1033, 1976.

12. WALLACE, S. J. Spontaneous fits after convulsions with fever. *Arch. Dis. Child.* 52:192-196, 1977.

13. WHITE, K. L., WILLIAMS, T. F., AND GREENBERG, B. G. The ecology of medical care. *N. Engl. J. Med.* 265:885-892, 1961.

FIVE

Study Design: The Experimental Approach

> *I took 12 patients in the scurvy . . . two of these were ordered each a quart of cider . . . Two others took 25 gutts of elixer vitriol . . . two took two spoonfuls of vinegar . . . two were put under a course of sea-water . . . two others had each two oranges and one lemon . . . two took the bigness of a nutmeg three-times-a-day. . . .*
> —James Lind, A Treatise of the Scurvy

Let us now sing the praises of the controlled trial! Although its ancestry certainly dates back to the eighteenth century, when James Lind fed 12 British sailors everything from sea water and vinegar to oranges (not limes) in an attempt to treat scurvy, wide acceptance of the experimental strategy is a recent occurrence. The British trials on the chemotherapy of tuberculosis performed in the early 1950s are by many accounts the birth of the modern fascination with the controlled trial. It represents the only study design available for clinical researchers that approximates the laboratory experiment. Most noted as a recipe for comparing drug therapies, the technique has evolved into a tool for evaluating a wide variety of clinical problems. Examples include the use of the controlled trial to compare methods of childbirth, study medical versus surgical treatment of coronary artery disease, and assess relaxation and meditation as a means of reducing high blood pressure. The scope of the

design has broadened to include what are strictly speaking nonclini-
cal areas of concern, such as, health services, education, and health
administration. Trials have been created to evaluate the efficacy of
nurse practitioners compared with physicians and judge the effectiveness of campaigns promoting the use of seat belts. There are a
growing number of aficionados who would subject every therapeutic maneuver to the scrutiny of the controlled trial before it is
loosed on the public.

Certainly after dealing with the frustrating biases of the round-
about strategies of case-control and follow-up observational studies,
the controlled trial presents a refreshing, direct approach. The many
difficulties of studying populations in their free-living state appear to
be obviated by the planned comparisons of drugs or surgical techniques, health-education programs, or administrative innovations
that are possible with the controlled trial design. Life for researchers is
much simpler when they have some control over interventions.
Nevertheless, there are chinks in the armor of the controlled trial that
medical readers must know about. We will look at four major areas of
methodologic concern. The first of these has to do with entry criteria
and how people get into the study. Next we will scrutinize the intervention or treatment itself: whether it is reproducible, practical, and
free of bias. The pitfalls of selecting a comparison population is a
third area of concern with some problems reminiscent of the case-
control and follow-up designs. Finally, we will explore an area that is
unique to the controlled trial, that of subject allocation, and see how
bias can occur when placing subjects into experimental groups. For
those who become intrigued with the subject, excellent commentaries are available from Hill [12], Sackett [19], and Elwood [6].

Subjects: Who Gets In

The Study Population

As we've seen in discussing other study designs, the
people an investigator chooses to study make a big difference. If
relaxation therapy truly lowers blood pressure in a middle-class private practice, will it also work in an inner-city clinic? Will a new
learning program developed for medical students at a large midwest-

ern medical school be transferrable to a small school on the east coast? Experimental studies are just as susceptible to population-selection problems as observational designs.

An example comes from recent literature evaluating the use of single doses of antibiotics for treatment of urinary-tract infections [7]. The goal of these experiments was to improve therapy for women with cystitis by demonstrating that a single dose of three grams of amoxicillin was as effective as the conventional therapy of ten days of the same antibiotic. If single-dose therapy proved effective, thousands of practitioners and patients who are confronted with this common problem would benefit. The investigators went to some lengths to differentiate between women with cystitis or lower-tract infection and those who had pyelonephritis or more serious upper-urinary-tract disease. Patients were excluded if they had fevers greater than 38°C, rigors, flank pain, or appeared toxic, so clinically they all appeared to have cystitis. Further, a special fluorescent antibody-coated bacterial assay was performed on urine specimens obtained from each subject. The presence of antibody-coated bacteria suggests tissue invasion of the kidneys and was used as an indicator of upper-tract infection; non-antibody-coated bacteria were taken to indicate a superficial infection of the bladder.

As the authors suspected, the success of single-dose amoxicillin varied with the presence or absence of antibody coating (see table 5–1). Investigators found that single-dose therapy was just as effec-

Table 5–1 Response of Urinary-Tract Infections, Defined by the Results of the Antibody-Coated Bacteria Assay, to Single-Dose and Conventional Therapy with Amoxicillin

Assay Result	Therapy[a]	No. of Patients	No. of Relapses[b]
Negative	Single dose	22	0
Negative	Conventional	21	0
Positive	Conventional	18	9

Adapted from Fang, et al. L. S. T. [7] by permission of the *New England Journal of Medicine*, 298:414, 1978.

[a]Single dose = 3 grams; conventional = 250 mg 4 times/day.
[b]One week after completion of therapy.

tive as the standard ten-day course for women who had lower-tract infections. All 22 patients who had non-antibody-coated bacteria and were given single-dose therapy showed symptomatic improvement within two days. Women who had lower-tract disease and were given conventional therapy had similar good results. However, for 18 patients whose infections were caused by antibody-coated bacteria, results were much less encouraging. Relapse rates were high even after conventional treatment. With almost a third of patients who appeared clinically to have uncomplicated cystitis turning out to be unsuitable candidates for single-dose treatment, the value of the new therapy for clinicians is questionable at best.

A subsequent paper by the same group of investigators supplied further insight into the problem [18]. The original study population had been selected from ambulatory patients of the Massachusetts General Hospital, a well-known, big-city referral center. To add to the experience with single-dose treatment, the investigators shared their protocol with two other sites in a "multicenter trial." Again, the efficacy of single-dose amoxicillin therapy for nonantibody-coated bacterial infections was demonstrated. And again, one-third of patients were found to have antibody-coated bacteria. However, there was a marked difference in the rates of fluorescing bacteria among the three institutions. One of the new sites, Parkland Memorial Hospital, had a frequency of just over 60%; the other new site, Kaiser-Permanente Health Program in Oregon, showed a rate of only 8%. That is a big difference. It suggests that different populations were being selected for study. A fascinating final bit of information the authors glean from this multicenter effort is that antibody-coating appears to be related to the duration of a woman's symptoms. The average length of symptoms prior to therapy was almost six days for women with antibody-coated bacteria compared with two days for those in whom the assay was negative. Women in the prepaid health plan are middle-class, have easy access to the medical system, come in for care early, show a low rate of antibody coating, and respond well to single-dose therapy. Patients at Parkland are ". . . of low socioeconomic means, without easy access to medical care, coming to the emergency ward of a municipal hospital . . ." They have been sick longer, come to treatment with a much higher proportion of recalcitrant organisms, and are much less suitable candidates for single-dose treatment. Does single-dose amoxicillin effectively treat urinary-tract infections? It depends on the patient population.

Entry Criteria

Having assessed the source and general make-up of the study population, the next question posed should be, "Is the diagnosis accurate?" Do the people that the investigator wishes to treat really have obesity, high blood pressure, or nonspecific vaginitis? Could you recognize a patient who qualifies for the intervention under discussion? How pedestrian! Of course the patient must have the illness to be included. That is only common sense. But it is dismaying to realize how often the report of a study fails to clearly define the criteria used for subject selection. The clinician must be able to identify and classify patients in the same manner as the experimenter. It is the same song of generalizability sung earlier, but it remains vital. If the investigator's definition of the problem varies markedly from your own or is unclear, you may be unable to utilize the new diet therapy, blood-pressure-reducing relaxation technique, or vaginal cream. You need to know whether hypertension was defined using the fourth or fifth Korotokoff sound and how many readings were taken before the diagnosis was made or whether vaginitis was diagnosed from symptoms alone, from microscopic examination of discharge, or by using cultures.

The internal validity of a trial can also be influenced by failure to adhere to clearly defined and appropriate entry criteria. Suppose a new antiarrhythmic drug has just come onto the market. For want of a better, generic name we will call it Nofib. Some colleagues have tested the drug against a placebo in 100 patients admitted to the coronary-care unit for myocardial infarction (MI). The goal of their experiment is to see whether Nofib protects against sudden death. We have been asked to review the results of their experiment. "The data," they sigh, "do not look encouraging." As depicted in table 5–2, you are inclined to agree. Of the 50 patients who received Nofib, 6 died, against 10 deaths in the comparison group. This difference, while favoring the experimental medication, is only eight percentage points and, according to a statistician hired for the occasion, is not statistically significant. It appears the investigators have come up empty-handed.

Table 5-2 Effects of Nofib on Survival of Patients with Myocardial Infarction[a] (N = 100)

	Nofib (%)	Control (%)
Survived	44	40
Died	6 (12)	10 (20)
Total	50	50

[a]As diagnosed by physician impression.

Could problems at the point of entry have contributed to this disappointing result?

"How," we ask, "were patients selected for the study?"

"Chosen randomly from all patients admitted to the coronary-care unit with suspected myocardial infarction," comes the reply.

"What were the entry criteria?"

"The attending physician's impression of a probable heart attack."

"What cardiographic, radiologic, and serum enzyme evidence was used in determining the diagnosis?"

"It varied, depending on each admitting physician's clinical judgment."

Unfortunately, much as we revere the clinical judgment of our colleagues, general impressions and ever-present gut feelings are not acceptable entry criteria for a study. Many more people are admitted to coronary-care units for suspected or possible heart attacks than actually sustain infarctions. At least in the short term, the prognosis for persons not infarcting is more favorable than for those who have an MI. If a substantial number of entrants into the study are misclassified as having had heart attacks, the beneficial effects of Nofib may be substantially diluted. Comparison of table 5-2 and table 5-3 illustrates how inadequate diagnosis might influence the results. Based on the original data (table 5-2), only 8 in every 100 patients (20% minus 12%) would be expected to benefit from treatment. Suppose, however, that 50 percent of the patients entered into the study were incorrectly classified. Let us also assume that survival for

Table 5-3 Effects of Nofib on Survival of Patients with Myocardial Infarction[a] (N = 50)

	Nofib (%)	Control (%)
Survived	19	15
Died	6 (24)	10 (40)
Total	25	25

[a]Redefined by symptoms, ECG, and serum-enzyme criteria.

the patients who do not have MI is good and that mortality occurs only among patients who really sustain heart attacks. When misclassified subjects are removed from the pool, results appear quite different (table 5-3). The death rate among patients given Nofib has risen to 24 percent, but the corresponding rate for patients given placebo is 40 percent. The difference in survivorship has doubled to 16 percent. Although it is possible this difference is due to chance rather than a result of Nofib (as we will discuss in chapter 8), misclassification has caused an underestimate of success.

Methods of Classification

Criteria for entry into the study must be clearly stated and must constitute an acceptable definition of the disease. Methods used to classify people must also be reasonable. A problem occurs whenever sophisticated technical equipment or laboratory procedures that are not available to most practitioners are required to identify subjects who will benefit from therapy.

The work on single-dose antibiotic treatment of urinary-tract infections is a case in point. The antibody-coated bacterial assay used for the studies is not a simple procedure. Urine specimens must be centrifuged and the resulting sediments washed twice in buffered saline. Washed sediments are then treated with fluorescein (conjugated antihuman globulin), incubated for thirty minutes, and then rewashed twice. Smears are prepared from this mixture and examined under a microscope that is specially equipped to detect fluorescence. Not exactly the kind of test available to every home and office do-it-yourselfer. Since we have already decided we only want to administer single-dose treatment to women who do not have fluorescent bacteria (lower-tract disease) we have reached an impasse. In populations where the frequency of antibody-coated infections is high, we must be willing to risk initiating inadequate treatment of a substantial portion of our patients, or we must continue to employ conventional therapy. Fancy technology has done us in.

A similar problem occurred in a British trial evaluating therapy for hemorrhoids [13]. In this study, the authors compared a number of treatments such as anal dilatation, sphincterotomy, rubber-band ligation, and high-fiber diet. However, before patients were assigned to the different therapies, they were divided into two groups: those having "high maximal resting anal pressure" and those having "low maximal resting anal pressure." This elegant classification was determined by means of a water-filled balloon probe and manometer. Again, we have a bit of technology that is outside the experience of most clinicians; and as with the antibody-coated bacteria, the success of the treatment offered to hemorrhoid sufferers turns out to depend on correctly classifying them as high- or low-pressure patients.

For clinicians who lack water-filled balloon probes, these authors offer some assistance—clinical guidelines that help distinguish high-pressure from low-pressure hemorrhoids. The high-pressure group is characterized as "young people, usually men, whose principle symptom is bleeding and anal discomfort." "Older patients, usually women, in whom prolapse is the principle complaint" usually have low anal pressures. This information is helpful and is a feature that should be sought by readers evaluating clinical trials. When a special laboratory test or technologic instrument is used to classify patients and this classification is important to results, the author must provide *practical* guidelines for making this same distinction. Investigators who are mindful of the clinician's need to function with materials that are readily at hand will supply reproducible suggestions for classifying patients.

In this report of a study evaluating treatments of nonspecific vaginitis, investigators used special culture techniques for isolating the bacterium that is presumed to be responsible for the disease [16]. Very few physicians' offices or hospital laboratories would possess the capabilities to grow and identify this organism. Furthermore, waiting for the culture to grow and for biochemical tests necessary for proper identification to be performed would take days and waste therapeutic time. These authors save the day by offering several reproducible alternatives to classify patients with bacterial vaginitis.

First they give a detailed description of the appearance, odor, and characteristics of the bacteria-induced discharge. Then they provide a mini-experiment within the study to show that a microscopic examination of discharge to detect clue cells provides a good proxy for cultures.

To assess the problem of subject selection, ask the following as you sort through the methodology of the controlled trial:

1. Where does the study population come from? Are they referred to specialty centers or are they typical of primary care patients? Do they represent a spectrum of disease or a selected slice of the range of a given illness?

2. Are criteria for entry spelled out? Do the patients under study all have the disease they are supposed to have and are the author's definitions of that disease reasonable?

3. Are the techniques used for classifying subjects practical and reproducible? If methods are used that are beyond the reach of most clinicians, are suitable proxy measures offered?

The Intervention or Treatment

Having scrutinized characteristics of the patients under study, let us turn attention to the treatment or intervention itself. Therapies being offered should be carefully defined, reproducible, and make practical sense. As we have seen before, principles that may seem self-evident are frequently ignored.

Practicality

The clinician always has the right to ask, "Is the treatment under consideration practical?" Sometimes the academicians who test these things become so involved in the intricacies of their business, they forget about some real-world constraints. When a group of investigators created an experiment to test a method for preventing travelers' diarrhea [4], it looked as if they had come on a good thing. By giving bismuth subsalicylate prophylactically to a group of students on tour in Mexico, the authors were able to demonstrate a 60 percent reduction in the occurrence of tourista. Since bismuth subsalicylate comes in several well-tolerated, over-the-counter preparations, it looked as if these results had much to offer to voyagers of the world. Alas, a small hitch! The medication tested comes as a suspension, and the dosage evaluated was two ounces taken four times each day. To achieve the desired prophylactic effect, it was calculated that a tourist visiting abroad for three weeks would need to carry a total supply of 168 ounces, or 21 bottles, of the medication [11]. The total weight of this precaution amounts to over 20 pounds leaving the average traveler with a very heavy suitcase and little room for souvenirs. Do not get buffaloed by the ballyhooing of the experts. If a fancy treatment is not realistic, it does not matter how successful it is reported to be.

Bias

A most intriguing problem with treatments offered in controlled trials relates to compliance bias. Feinstein [8] has written about this subject and offers a number of subtle variations on the theme. Compliance bias can operate when dissimilarities in the treatments being compared create differing rates of patient adherence to the methods. If one of the therapies is a diet that is particularly difficult to follow or a medicine that tastes dreadful, study results may suggest lack of efficacy when, in fact, the explanation for the poor result is that patients failed to follow the therapy.

A good case for compliance bias can be made in the study evaluating alternative treatments for hemorrhoids [13]. Recall that in the study several surgical procedures were compared to a high-fiber diet as approaches to this troublesome condition. Diet therapy faired poorly in the comparisons as table 5–4 illustrates. At a 12-month follow-up, 74 percent of high-pressure patients who underwent anal dilatation were improved compared to only 27 percent of diet subjects; among low-pressure patients, rubber-band ligation gave 82 percent of subjects relief with only 28 percent of dieters reporting success. It is possible, however, that the results reflect a compliance bias. Surgery has an aura of purposeful completion about it. We have reason to expect that the surgical procedures were carried out as advertised. Patients allocated to the diet group, on the other hand, were simply given a "high roughage diet instruction sheet and a one month supply of bran tablets." No fanfare and no follow-up to see how well they adhered to the diet. From what we know of medical-compliance problems in general and unattractive diets in particular, it

Table 5–4 Clinical Results 12 Months After Treatment of Hemorrhoids by Surgical Procedures and Diet

	High-Pressure Group (n = 108)			Low-Pressure Group (n = 108)		
	Anal Dilatation (n = 37)	Sphincterotomy (n = 34)	Diet (n = 37)	Rubber-Band Ligation (n = 35)	Cryosurgery (n = 36)	Diet (n = 37)
Asymptomatic	11	6	5	16	4	4
Improved	14	6	5	7	10	5
No better	5	12	13	3	7	10
Required other treatment	4	9	14	2	11	13
No follow-up data available	3	1	0	7	4	5

Adapted from Keighley, M. R. B., et al. [13].

is reasonable to suspect that a number of patients failed to follow the plan.

The study on treatment of nonspecific vaginitis offers another example where differential rates of compliance may create a bias [16]. Among the therapies offered to women with vaginitis were a sulfonamide cream that was to be inserted vaginally twice daily for ten days and a pill to be taken twice a day for seven. Use of the cream is a messy business and proper application is difficult. When the results of this study indicate the failure of the cream compared with the pills, one must wonder whether the ineffectiveness of the cream is not partly due to compliance problems.

Poor compliance can also obscure results of a clinical trial when the treatments under study have similar rates of adherence. If overall rates of compliance are low for all methods under scrutiny, beneficial effects of any of the agents may be masked. Treatment of high blood pressure has always been plagued by compliance problems; people just will not take their pills. Suppose we are trying to compare a new antihypertensive agent to one of the standard treatments available. Both medications are tablets that are taken twice daily. Neither medication has an offensive taste or intolerable side effects. In other words, we anticipate no difference in compliance. However, it turns out the patients we are studying are very relaxed about taking their prescribed medications. When it comes time to look at the results, we find little improvement in the control of high blood pressure among patients taking the new agent compared with the old therapy. However, we also discover that only 20 percent of patients took their pills regularly. Under these circumstances it is very difficult to know whether or not the drug under study has an effect. As in the Nofib example where medication effects were diluted by including improperly diagnosed heart-attack patients, low overall compliance may hide a real benefit.

Of course, the compliance issue can be viewed from another perspective. While one may argue that an unpalatable diet or noxious medicine cannot be dismissed as ineffective until we have assured ourselves that noncompliance has been controlled, noncompliance is a reality. It exists as a practical impediment in day-to-day medical care. The clinical trial that includes noncompliers may give a more accurate picture of the value of an intervention in the real world. Patients are going to have difficulty using vaginal cream properly, following rigorous diets, or lugging 20 pounds of Pepto-Bismol to Mexico. Authors who acknowledge and analyze potential compliance problems are more help to the clinician than those who simply exclude nonadherent patients from consideration or take heroic steps to make sure that patients follow instructions.

Competing Interventions

While we are contemplating the treatments used by investigators, we should consider the possibility that cointerventions are occurring. A cointervention, as the names implies, is another, usually unrecognized, form of treatment that is taking place at the same time as the intervention under study. A cointervention may play a major role in achieving the results but receives no credit. To bias results of the study, cointerventions must not only be responsible for the effects observed but be unevenly distributed between treatment groups. Suppose we were looking for evidence that anticoagulants given to patients recuperating from myocardial infarction prevented thromboembolic disease and reduced mortality. Patients with heart attacks are assigned to two different units within the hospital. In one they receive anticoagulant therapy and the other, none. We find at the conclusion of our trial that there were significantly fewer deaths among patients in the anticoagulation group. But just as we are about to sound the fanfare and publish our results, we discover that patients admitted to the unit that was administering anticoagulants also received prophylactic antiarrhythmic agents and had early ambulation. These are cointerventions that may boast partial or total responsibility for the improved mortality seen in our experimental unit.

Cointerventions may be a factor in the trial evaluating the therapies for hemorrhoids [13]. Patients receiving surgical procedures, for example, may be administered adjunct treatments that impact on their outcome. Postoperative patients are commonly prescribed topical ointments, sitz baths, pharmacologic stool softeners, and often are encouraged to use bran and high-roughage diets. The use of any of these additional treatments would render interpretation even more difficult.

Subtler forms of cointervention occur. Patients in a hypertension study may appear to be responding satisfactorily to a new antihypertensive medication, when in fact they are part of a group whose blood pressure is monitored by a sympathetic nurse. The supportive manner of the nurse may have a stronger effect on reducing blood pressure than the pill in question. If this nurse happens to be taking blood pressures for only one group of subjects in a comparative study, a cointervention bias is created.

A number of characteristics of the intervention, then, must be carefully considered:

1. Is it clearly defined so as to be reproducible in other settings? Are dosages and details of techniques stated and consistent with current practices?

2. Are the methods under examination practical? Could treatments be used in a variety of medical settings or are they suitable only for the fantasy world of academics?

3. Is there a potential for compliance bias? Are treatments under study sufficiently different in application that differential rates of adherence are likely? If so, has the author addressed this issue and attempted to assess actual compliance for the interventions?

4. Are competing interventions occurring? If so, are they unequally distributed among treatment groups? Has the author looked for these and tried to assess their potential impact?

Controls: Their Presence and Comparability

Though it seems condescending to mention it, a glance to make sure that a controlled trial contains a concurrent control group is always worthwhile. Most studies nowadays evaluate a control or comparison group at the same time that they test their subjects. Comparison subjects may be given placebos, alternate treatments, or nothing at all. When authors decide that the success of their experiment will be so obvious that a comparison group is unnecessary, watch out! The suggestive power of thinking that you are receiving a medical treatment or innovative educational program is enormous. Remember the experience of treating angina by ligation of the internal mammary arteries discussed in chapter 2. Until a side-by-side comparison group received a sham operation, this surgical technique was thought to be highly successful.

Another example of the placebo effect is demonstrated in two papers that assess treatment of diabetic neuropathy with the drug, phenytoin. In 1968, an article reported a highly successful experiment utilizing this commonly used anticonvulsant to relieve pain among diabetics suffering from peripheral nerve problems [5]. The results were exciting! The investigator reported that 68% of the patients showed excellent symptomatic relief with a "fair response" in another 17 percent. Appealing as these results appear, a red flag should flutter at the realization that the study is totally without a comparison group. When the experiment was repeated some years later [20], investigators not only included a control group that received a placebo capsule but alternated, or crossed over, the subjects. This means that the same patients received alternating courses of the active drug, phenytoin, and the placebo and charted their symptoms without the knowledge of which preparation they were taking.[1] Under the pressure of this carefully constructed experiment, the benefits of phenytoin collapsed.

The presence of just any comparison group is not sufficient. Ideally, controls should be selected from the same parent population as subjects who receive the intervention. Controls taken from a different patient population or chosen from an earlier period in time may not be suitable. Let us look at several examples where comparability may not have been achieved.

The first of these studies compares two estrogen preparations that were evaluated as postcoital contraceptives [3]. The study took place at five different centers, including student health services and affiliates of planned-parenthood programs. Some 1,300 women who came seeking contraception after unprotected intercourse were given one of two estrogen preparations. In analyzing the efficacy of this after-the-fact contraception, the authors compared the two different estrogens and found a small difference in pregnancy rates. No problems in this comparison. However, in an attempt to judge the overall effectiveness of postcoital contraception, they skate onto some thinner ice. Since no untreated control group was included in the original design, they compare pregnancy rates of women given estrogens to "expected pregnancy rates for one unprotected act of intercourse." These estimates are derived from other studies and turn out to be about 7/100 or 7 percent: substantially higher than the rate of only 1 percent determined for women who get the morning-after treatment. The question is whether the expected fertility rates of comparison subjects are the same as those of women coming to student health services for postcoital contraception? Chances are they are not. Estimates of pregnancy risk for the postcoital study group are based on reports supplied by the woman about her last menstrual period, when she had intercourse, and the assumption that most women ovulate fourteen days prior to the onset of their menstrual period. One comparison study bases the risk of conception on data from 241 couples of "proven fertility who were experienced in using the basal body temperature method for regulating their fertility;" another comparison study group was comprised of married women with "presumed normal reproductive capacity" who were part of a program in artificial insemination. Now it might seem that a group of married women who are trying hard to get pregnant and carefully monitoring their ovulatory cycles would be quite different from a group of anxious young women who are seeking redress from a misadventure. These kinds of differences make it difficult to make a meaningful comparison between the rate of pregnancy in women receiving estrogens and their historic controls.

The authors of the study recognized that their source populations were different, so they demonstrated that for three different populations used as comparisons, pregnancy rates are remarkably similar. This gives us at least a suggestion that their estimate of natural fertility rates may be valid. It does not, however, allay our concern that with the anxiety and recall problems of the student health service patients, expected fertility rates for this subgroup may be considerably less than 7% even before postcoital contraception.

Another study that suffers from the lack of a comparable control group attempts to evaluate the benefits of an exercise program on reducing mortality among patients who have suffered heart attack [17]. In this study, 68 male volunteers under 51 years of age who had sustained a myocardial infarction (MI) at least five months earlier were enrolled in an exercise program. Controls were selected from medical records of patients diagnosed as having heart attack who would have been eligible for entry into the program but who, "for a variety of reasons did not join." The investigators came up with "matched controls" who were similar in age and number of previous infarctions to the exercise group. Results, as shown in table 5–5, were quite impressive. The exercised patients had substantially fewer recurrent MIs and only half as many cardiac deaths as the control group.

Unfortunately, the adequacy of this control group is up for debate. Why did these men who were eligible for the exercise program not participate? Reading back we find that reasons included "family physician disapproval, shift work, lack of interest, or simply unawareness that such a program existed." Careful! One must strongly suspect that patients with a lack of interest are a very different breed from their exercising contemporaries. The authors themselves recognize this potential shortcoming and suggest that "subjects who enter a rehabilitation program voluntarily may differ psychologically from those who do not in a way that might effect prognosis" and that, "subjects who enter a rehabilitation program frequently stop smoking and lose weight." The reduced morbidity and mortality seen in the exercisers may be due not to the experimental program but to other disparities between the compared groups that are risk factors for heart disease.

Subjects used as comparisons in controlled trials should ideally come from the same population and be studied at the same time as subjects receiving the intervention. If there are likely to be differences in the groups under study, authors should make an effort to alert us to that possibility and provide what evidence they can muster to support similarity. Usually there is some demographic information available on subjects with which to do this. Many articles will provide a table or list comparing features like age, sex, parity, education, and so on, so readers may judge for themselves how similar the groups appear to be. Even then comparability among trial groups is not guaranteed.

Allocation: Subject Assignment

Random Allocation

Subjects must be allocated by the investigators. This is the activity that gives the controlled trial its special shine, but it also offers yet another opportunity for biases to slip in to tarnish the results. While many people speak of the randomized controlled trial as if the term were all one word, random allocation of subjects is only one technique in use. As the term "random" gets tossed about rather casually, it is worth reminding ourselves precisely what it means. Randomly assigning subjects does not mean that the investigator grabs everyone sitting on the north side of the waiting room and

Table 5-5   Recurrence and Death from Myocardial Infarction in Exercise Subjects and Controls

	Nonfatal Recurrence	Cardiac Death
	n = 66	
Exercise Subjects	2 (3%)	5 (8%)
	n = 117	
Controls	13 (11%)	24 (19%)

Adapted from Rechnitzer, P. A., et al. [17].

plops them into Group A, leaving folks sitting on the south side to form Group B. The goal of proper subject allocation is avoiding selection bias that might create unwanted differences in comparative groups. People might congregate on the north side of the waiting room because the chairs are softer there and easier on their arthritic joints or because their friends from work sit there. Systematic differences between these people and their counterparts on the other side of the waiting room may affect results of the study. The problem is cut of the same cloth as the convenience sampling discussed in chapter 4. Convenience allocation opens the way to bias. While it may be done with best intentions of being unselective, problems can occur.

Random allocation, on the other hand, is a very carefully planned method of assigning subjects that avoids bias. It may be accomplished by making assignments from a table of random numbers, using calculator programs that generate random numbers, or even drawing numbers from a hat; but for true random assignment to take place, subjects must have an equal chance of being assigned to any of the study groups at hand. Only by using this rigorous method of allocation can we guarantee against the unconscious biases of the assigning investigators and, indeed, the study subjects themselves.

An example of biased allocation comes from a study that attempted to assess the risks and benefits of delivering babies in a special birthing-room setting [10]. In this experiment, a group of 500 women was offered the chance to deliver in a "bedroom type room next to the delivery suite." Amenities included a queen-sized bed, casual furnishings, and a large, private bathroom. Also included in the birthing-room delivery plan was a series of agreements between patients and staff, which included avoidance of intravenous fluids, fetal monitors, excessive analgesia, and much of the paraphernalia associated with traditional in-hospital deliveries. The patients participating in this birthing-room experience were compared with a "similar number of low-risk mothers and babies in the standard delivery room." The results of the study suggest not only that the birthing room was safe but that deliveries occurring there had fewer complications for mother and baby than deliveries under standard conditions. The author evaluated 42 perinatal outcomes in the two groups and found that birthing-room deliveries had a significantly lower rate for 12 complications including cesarean sections, fetal distress, jaundice, congenital anomalies, and child abuse.

The author registers happy surprise at what he terms the "unexpected" results; but the reduced rate of complications in the experimental group is probably not unexpected. Let us review exactly how subjects were allocated to the birthing room and standard-care groups. Participants in the birthing-room deliveries were volunteers. They were assessed for risk factors and only low-risk subjects remained eligible for the study. Factors placing women into the standard-care group are not clearly specified except that these women were also said to be low-risk.

Are the groups comparable? Are the so-called risk factors that may influence the outcome of pregnancy equivalent in both? We know that the patients differ in one important respect: one group volunteered to participate in the birthing-room experiment while the other women did not wish to partake. Could this difference affect results? We are supplied with little information about characteristics of these two groups of women that might help us decide. However, we know enough about volunteers in health programs to make a guess that the birthing-room volunteers are probably somewhat older, better educated, and of higher socioeconomic status and parity than the comparison women. Since these factors are known to be associated with a favorable outcome of pregnancy, we again have a situation where the intervention, the birthing room, appears to produce lower complication rates when, in fact, improved outcomes are a manifestation of allocating a healthier group of women to the experimental group. Women interested in birthing rooms are likely to produce bigger, bouncier babies regardless of the type of delivery employed.

Had the author of this study randomly allocated only subjects who were willing to undergo the birthing-room experience, patient selection biases might have been avoided and the results been very different. An elegance of allocation is illustrated in a Canadian study on a similar subject [14]. Investigators in this report wished to explore the possible benefits of the Leboyer approach to childbirth, a method that promotes birth in a dark, quiet room, delayed clamping of the umbilical cord, and calming of the infant by massage and bathing in warm water. To guard against lack of comparability between the Leboyer and "conventional delivery" groups, all subjects were required to fulfill eligibility requirements that included a low obstetrical risk score and interest in the Leboyer approach to childbirth before they were entered in the study. Random assignment was then made so that each woman had an equal chance of being delivered by the Leboyer or the conventional method. As things turned out, the authors were unable to demonstrate any important advantage to soft lights and tepid baths when compared to a conventional albeit gentle delivery.

Even allocation methods that would appear to be free from bias can present problems. Gifford and Feinstein describe a fascinating example in discussing experiments evaluating the use of anticoagulants for myocardial infarction [9]. In a study performed in the late 1940s, patients admitted to hospital with the diagnosis of acute infarction were placed on anticoagulants or left untreated, depending on the day of the week. On odd days, patients received anticoagulants, on even days they served as controls. Although this system of allocation would seem a vast improvement over that described for the birthing-room experience, questions of bias were raised. Physicians who were admitting patients to these hospitals were aware of the nature of the study that was being conducted. They knew that if the date was even, their patients would go untreated. Such knowledge might sit poorly with a doctor who had already concluded that anticoagulants are beneficial. If it were the waning hours of June 16 and he had a patient in the emergency room who had chest pain but was not severely ill, the temptation would be great to let the hour of midnight slip by before admitting the patient to the ward. A slight delay in the emergency room could assure the patient of receiving the anticoagulant therapy.

How could this bias results? The outcome being evaluated in this experiment was mortality, and there are many factors other than anticoagulants that may affect a patient's survival following a heart attack. Among the best predictors of outcome are the severity of the heart attack and the patient's condition at the time of admission to hospital. The only patients for whom physicians could reasonably delay admission to gain access to the anticoagulant dates would be patients with less-severe illness. Patients in shock or with arrhythmias would not be good candidates for this bit of strategy; nor would they be good candidates for survival. So if a number of patients who were less ill and had a more favorable prognosis were systemically included in the anticoagulation group, survival would appear spuriously high and anticoagulants would garner undeserved praise for prolonging life. An intricate bit of business, but it may well have happened.

Even strict randomization in a clinical trial can fall prey to unexpected events. Investigators in another trial looking at anticoagulants and heart attack felt they were protecting themselves from bias by randomly assigning patients to receive heparin or serve as controls by a system of sealed envelopes [2]. To their dismay, they discovered that anticoagulant anarchists were having their way again and were transilluminating the envelopes to foil the random allocation.

Stratification. The foibles of human nature not withstanding, random allocation is the method of choice for controlled trials. But even when executed properly there is a risk that randomization will not accomplish its intended purpose. Random assignment attempts to equalize experimental and comparison groups by giving each subject an equal chance to be in any of the groups; but chance is chancy business as anyone who has flipped coins or played cards can avow. Just as it is possible to come up with heads for eight out of ten flips of the coin, so can groups assigned by the random process turn out to be dissimilar in their makeup. Even the best designed and best intentioned studies can hit upon bad luck. A large collaborative trial comparing methods of controlling diabetes was a well-publicized victim of this mischance [21]. Patients admitted to the University Group Diabetes Program were randomly allocated and received one of four diabetic therapies. Included in these were diet, insulin, and oral hypoglycemic agents. At the conclusion of the study a surprising discovery was made. Patients receiving oral agents showed a higher incidence of cardiovascular mortality than groups receiving the other treatments. This finding had alarming implications for the many patients already receiving these medications. However, when data were further analyzed it became apparent that the composition of the treatment groups was not comparable. Patients receiving oral agents had a higher rate of conditions predisposing to heart disease than subjects in other groups. The question becomes whether it is the medication or the unequal distribution of these predisposing factors that accounts for the increased mortality. The dilemma has consumed many journal pages and is still under debate [1,15].

Bias can occur any time groups being compared are unequal with respect to either risk factors that predispose to disease or existing illnesses that may influence outcome. While there are methods for dealing with unanticipated inequalities when data are analyzed, most investigators would rather not be victimized by the noncomparability problem to begin with. If important risk factors or comorbid conditions (concurrent illnesses that may influence outcome) can be identified at the outset, subjects may be grouped or prognostically stratified prior to assignment. Feinstein has written extensively about prognostic stratification and its importance in interpreting clinical trials [8].

In the Leboyer childbirth example, the investigators were savvy enough to use prognostic stratification to avoid the pitfalls of this multirisk situation. Before assignment, patients were grouped according to parity and social class, and random allocation proceeded separately within each subgroup. The likelihood that high-risk, first pregnancies end up being compared with less risky subsequent pregnancies because of chance maldistribution is thus minimized.

Summary

This all seems like a tremendous amount of effort to expend just looking at the methods of controlled trials, but by now certain of these principles should have a familiar ring. The problems of comparability of comparison subjects and the forces of selection that go into choosing exposed or experimental subjects have come up before in discussing case-control and follow-up designs. The principles are the same. The reader has a right to expect an author to supply the information necessary to generalize from the specific study to other populations. We can likewise expect that care has been used in selecting comparison subjects, and that when questions of comparability arise, the author will provide information about how subjects and their controls are similar and how they differ.

Although experimental designs, like follow-up studies, are not encumbered by recall bias and problems encountered in using data from the past, they share the plague of attrition. Both of these prospective designs depend upon following subjects over time to assess outcomes. The risk that patients will drop out of the project because they are depressed or are unable to comply with a complicated diet is a constant threat to results.

Comfort in assessing these methodological pitfalls comes only with practice—reading lots of studies and scouring the methodology for problems. But remember, flaw catching can become a disheartening addiction, since very few studies are free of blemish. If you look hard enough weakness may be found in the most robust of designs. We must guard against dismissing a study because of defects that are relatively unimportant. When flaws are found, we must ask whether the problems will impinge upon the validity of the study. In cases such as the birthing-room experiment where great potential for bias exists from the unequal distribution of risk factors in the two groups, the problem is crippling. After assessing this design one would do well to proceed to other reading tasks. In other cases, such as the case-control study of women with recurrent urinary-tract infections, recall bias, though a potential threat, probably did not have a major impact on results.

Investigators, like the rest of us, are subject to the imperfections of humanity. They concoct and serve up their studies with the best of intentions. Often the seasoning is not quite right and sometimes critical ingredients are missing or misapportioned. Have compassion for the cooks; try to distinguish between small matters of taste and major indigestibilities.

Notes

[1]Crossing patients over is a technique that is used commonly in drug trials. It has the advantages of (1) reducing the number of subjects required, since each subject serves as both an experimental subject and a control, and (2) lessening the biologic vari-

ability inherent in comparing different subjects by comparing each subject with himself.

References

1. BRADLEY, R. F., DOLGER, H., FORSHAM, P. H., AND SELTZER, H. Settling the UGDP controversy? *JAMA* 232:813–817, 1975.

2. CARLETON, R. A., SANDERS, C. A., AND BURACK, W. R. Heparin administration after acute myocardial infarction. *N. Engl. J. Med.* 263:1002–1004, 1960.

3. DIXON, G. W., SCHLESSELMAN, J. J., ORY, H. W., AND BLYE, R. P. Ethinyl estradiol and conjugated estrogens as postcoital contraceptives. *JAMA* 244:1336–1339,1980.

4. DUPONT, H. L., SULLIVAN, P., EVANS, D. G., ET AL. Prevention of traveler's diarrhea (emporiatic enteritis). Prophylactic administration of subsalicylate bismuth. *JAMA* 243:237–241, 1980.

5. ELLENBERG, M. Treatment of diabetic neuropathy with diphenylhydantoin. *N.Y. State J. Med.* 68:2653–2655, 1968.

6. ELWOOD, J. M. Interpreting clinical trial results: Seven steps to understanding. *Can. Med. Assoc. J.* 123:343–345, 1980.

7. FANG, L. S. T., TOLKOFF-RUBIN, N. E., AND RUBIN, R. H. Efficacy of single-dose and conventional amoxicillin therapy in urinary-tract infection localized by the antibody-coated bacteria technique. *N. Engl. J. Med.* 298:413–416, 1978.

8. FEINSTEIN, A. R. *Clinical Biostatistics.* St. Louis: C. V. Mosby Co., 1977.

9. GIFFORD, R. H. AND FEINSTEIN, A. R. A critique of methodology in studies of anticoagulant therapy for acute myocardial infarction. *N. Engl. J. Med.* 280:351–357, 1969.

10. GOODLIN, R. C. Low-risk obstetric care for low-risk mothers. *Lancet* 1:1017–1019, 1980.

11. GORBACH, S. L. How to avoid running with *Escherichia coli*. *JAMA* 243:260–261, 1980.

12. HILL, A. B. *Principles of Medical Statistics* (9th ed.). New York: Oxford University Press, 1971.

13. KEIGHLEY, M. R. B., BUCHMANN, P., MINERVINI, S., ARABI, Y., AND ALEXANDER-WILLIAMS, J. Prospective trials of minor surgical procedures and high-fibre diet for haemorrhoids. *Brit. Med. J.* 2:967–969, 1979.

14. NELSON, N. M., ENKIN, M. W., SAIGAL, S., BENNETT, K. J., MILNERT, R., AND SACKETT, D. L. A randomized clinical trial of the Leboyer approach to childbirth. *N. Engl. J. Med.* 302:655–660, 1980.

15. O'SULLIVAN, J. B. AND D'AGOSTINO, R. B. Decisive factors in the tolbutamide controversy. *JAMA* 232:825–829, 1975.

16. PHEIFER, T. A., FORSYTH, P. S., DURFEE, M. A., POLLOCK, H. M., AND HOLMES, K. K. Nonspecific vaginitis: Role of *Haemophilus vaginalis* and treatment with metronidazole. *N. Engl. J. Med.* 298:1429–1434, 1978.

17. RECHNITZER, P. A., PICKARD, H. A., PAIVIO, A. U., YUHASZ, M. S., AND CUNNINGHAM, D. Long-term follow-up study of survival and recurrence rates following myocardial infarction in exercising and control subjects. *Circulation* 45:853–856, 1972.

18. RUBIN, R. H., FANG, L. S. T., JONES, S. R., ET AL. Single-dose amoxicillin therapy for urinary tract infection: Multicenter trial using antibody-coated bacteria localization technique. *JAMA* 244:561–564, 1980.

19. SACKETT, D. L. Design, measurement and analysis in clinical trials. In J. Hirsch, J. F. Cade, A. S. Gallus, et al. (Eds.) *Platelets, Drugs and Thrombosis.* Basel: S. Karger, 1975.

20. SAUDEK, C. D., WERNS, S., AND REIDENBERG, M. M. Phenytoin in the treatment of diabetic symmetrical polyneuropathy. *Clin. Pharm. Ther.* 22:196–199, 1977.

21. SCHOR, S. The University Group Diabetes Program: A Statistician looks at the mortality results. *JAMA* 217:1671–1675, 1971.

SIX

Making Measurements

I am giddy; expectation whirls me round.
—Troilus and Cressida, *Act III, Scene II*

We have ruminated over study designs; tasted some problems, such as, selective recall, loss to follow-up, and compliance bias; and sampled several solutions, such as, matching, stratification, and random allocation. We are ready now to consider the implementation of these designs, that is, examine how measurements are made and data acquired. After struggling with the complexities of study methodologies, gathering data would seem a straightforward proposition. By now it should come as no surprise that there are problems in this domain as well.

When measurements are made and data are collected, errors can occur. Children are improperly measured or their heights are incorrectly plotted on the growth curve; a centrifuged hematocrit tube is not correctly read; items on a personality-inventory scale are inadvertently left blank or filled in incorrectly. The list of unfortunate possibilities is almost endless, and the chance that data acquired by researchers do not properly measure the attributes they wish to determine is a potent hazard. Although errors in data collection can occur anywhere in the process—from obtaining measurements on a patient, through keypunching data cards for computer analysis—we will focus on problems that occur at the interface between patients and investigators. It is here that the most serious errors occur and the only point at which readers have a shot at detecting difficulties. We will discuss two general types of errors, those that occur in a random or unpredictable fashion and those that are made in a biased, systematic way.

Reliability and Validity

Two terms that readers will encounter whenever measurements are mentioned are validity and reliability. We have already discussed the concept of validity as it applies to the overall acceptance of study results (whether conclusions are justified based on design and interpretation) or in the case of external validity (whether results can be generalized to settings outside those described in the study). As used to describe data, validity refers to the degree to which a measurement represents a true value, such as, how closely a blood-pressure determination represents a patient's true blood pressure or a hematocrit estimates the actual packed cell volume. Reliability relates to the reproducibility of measurements. How closely do repeated measurements on the same subject agree? Both these attributes are important to clinical studies and are related. Errors can be caused by either a lack of validity or reliability. If six student nurses attempt to measure a patient's blood pressure and obtain values that range from 110/70 to 145/95, the results lack reliability. This creative group of estimates may be due to changes in the patient's anxiety level, differences in inflation of the cuff, or variable auditory acuity among the students. The results also lack validity. Better reproducibility is necessary to achieve a valid result but does not guarantee it. If a cuff of the wrong size is employed or the manometer is out of calibration, each of our six nurses might come up with a blood pressure reading of 145/95, a totally reliable finding, that does not represent the true pressure.

Observer Errors of the Unsystematic Sort

Over the past thirty to forty years we have begun to appreciate an amazing spectrum of variability that occurs when health researchers or health providers attempt to make clinical measurements. Problems of reliability pervade every aspect of clinical work from history taking and the physical examination to laboratory and x-ray investigations. Observers assessing the same patient, the same symptom, the same skin rash, or the same blood smear frequently come up with differing interpretations.

Cochrane et al. describe an example that occurred when British coalminers were being interviewed for symptoms of respiratory disease [3]. Some 900 men were divided into four groups for interview. Although not strictly randomized, the men queued up in a fashion that suggested that the groups being questioned were similar in composition. Physician interviewers obtained a standard history regarding symptoms, such as, cough, sputum production, pain in the chest, shortness of breath, and history of respiratory diseases. Figure 6–1 illustrates the variation of responses. Responses to what would appear to be an objective symptom like sputum production varied in frequency from as low as 13 percent by observer A to 42 percent for D—a remarkable disparity. This variability was variable, however. Although observer D found more sputum production and pain, observer C came up with more coughers, and observer B reported the highest rate of dyspnea.

When Medalie and colleagues were gathering information on a population of 10,000 adult males in the Israel Ischemic Heart Disease project, they encountered similar problems [10]. When a history of chest pain was elicited by pairs of physicians at three different examination sites, substantial variation was noted (*see* table 6–1). Pairs of observers elicited histories of no chest pain that differed by as much as 20 percentage points.

Measurements made in the course of the physical examination are equally prone to observer variability. In a study by Derryberry on "the reliability of medical judgments on malnutrition" [6], six pediatricians were asked to independently examine 108 eleven-year-old boys and rate their nutritional status. Each boy was examined by each physician and rated on a four point scale that ranged from "excellent" to "poor." In the author's understated prose, "the results of this investigation were disconcerting." Ratings of the six physicians showed marked variation. One physician rated 15 of the 108 boys as having poor nutritional status, another rated only two in that category. Twenty-five different boys were given the "poor" rating by at least one of the doctors, and only one child received a unanimous judgment of poor by the entire group of evaluators. Two youngsters received every rating from excellent through poor in the course of the six evaluations.

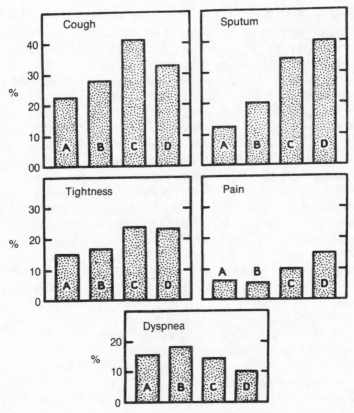

Figure 6–1. *Symptoms found by each of four observers interviewing approximately 200 men. (From Cochrane, A. L. et al. [3] by permission.)*

Even elements of the physical examination that would pretend high objectivity are subject to observer variability. Meade et al. report on differences between three physicians of "comparable clinical experience" who were given the task of palpating the peripheral pulses of 84 hospitalized patients [9]. For this experiment the examiners had only to record whether the pulse was present or absent. To spice up the game, 12 of the patients were recycled through the examination so that they were evaluated twice by each of the three observers. Table 6–2 summarizes some of the findings from this study. Agreement ranged from as high as 97% for palpation of femoral pulses to as

Table 6-1   Reports of Chest Pain Assessed by Six Physicians at Three Different Centers

	Number of Subjects Examined	Percent with Definite Angina	Percent with No Chest Pain
Center A			
Physician 1	214	1.9	71.5
Physician 2	229	5.7	55.9
Center B			
Physician 1	213	0.9	72.3
Physician 2	235	1.7	93.2
Center C			
Physician 1	238	4.6	66.4
Physician 2	240	4.6	67.0

Adapted from Medalie, J. H., et al. [10] by permission of the Israel Medical Association, P.O. Box 6, Jerusalem 91020, Israel.

low as 69% for the dorsalis pedis. If this interobserver problem was not bad enough, the 12 patients who underwent a second pulse check highlighted further deficiencies. Intraobserver error, that is, a rater's change from a previous assessment, also occurred. When the three examiners were checked on the 48 pulses that they assessed on two occasions, they changed their minds about the presence or absence of a pulse from 13% to 27% of the time (*see* table 6–3).

The pronouncements of those who interpret the technologic trappings of medicine are not immune from the problems of observer variation. Lack of agreement among experts reading coronary angiograms [7], electrocardiograms [4], and radiographs [1] has been demonstrated. In 1947, a group of investigators wished to compare the effectiveness of four different radiographic techniques for use in tuberculosis case-finding programs [1]. Their strategy was simply to take radiographs of the same patients using the different methods and have the films interpreted by a group of experts, in this case, five members of the Veteran's Administration Board of Roentgenology. While the investigators suspected that differences in interpretation would occur in the course of the study, they were surprised by the magnitude of the variability problem. For 1,200 radiographs that

Table 6-2 Agreement of Three Observers Examining Femoral, Posterior Tibial, and Dorsalis Pedis Pulses in 96 Male Patients

| | Agreement | Disagreement | | Agreement | Percent |
	Present, 3 Observers	Present, 2 Observers; Absent, 1 Observer	Present, 1 Observer; Absent, 2 Observers	Absent, 3 Observers	Total Agreement
Femoral (192 pulses)	187	4	1	0	97
Posterior tibial (192 pulses)	126	27	13	26	79
Dorsalis pedis (192 pulses)	105	29	30	28	69

Adapted from Meade, T. W., et al. [9] with permission.

Table 6-3 Intraobserver Variability in Recording Posterior Tibial and Dorsalis Pedis Pulses in Twelve Patients

Observer	Number of individual pulses found present on one examination and absent on another (48 pulses)
A	8/48 (17%)
B	6/48 (13%)
C	13/48 (27%)

From Meade, T. W., et al. [9] with permission.

were read independently by each of the five observers, the number of interpretations that were positive for tuberculosis ranged from 56 to 100. Again, there was no uniform agreement as to which these cases were, with 131 different films interpreted as positive by one or more of the readers. Intraobserver problems were also demonstrated as films were reread and observers changed their interpretations from previous readings. As it all turned out, observer consistency proved to be such a problem that the comparison of the four radiologic techniques became a secondary issue. The variability of observers posed a greater limitation to accurate diagnosis than the x-ray method utilized.

The catalog of observer problems should strike a concordant note with clinicians. Everyone experiences measurement disagreements, as any medical student who failed to palpate the 2-cm liver edge or hear the systolic heart murmur that the senior resident or attending physician uncovered can attest. We should realize however, that experience does not grant immunity from the problem. In the examples we have just discussed, the variant observers were often experts in their field. They have as much trouble as the rest of us.

Most of the errors we have been discussing occur in a haphazard or unpredictable fashion. They can be a nuisance since without reasonable measurement reliability the validity of study results will be compromised, but minor, random variations tend to even out—some higher and some lower—and human imperfectibility being what it is, can never be entirely eliminated.

Systematic Observer Error

There are, however, more dangerous brands of observer error. They occur when variations in measurements take on a predictable or biased aspect. An example comes from a study devised to determine the accuracy of clinical measurements of fetal heart rates [5]. In this investigation an electronic monitor was attached to record the intrauterine heart rate. At the same time members of the hospital staff counted the heart beats by auscultation. Observer variations in the range of 20% of the monitored rate were discovered. However, the pattern of this variability did not occur randomly. Fetal heart rate is a guide to the infant's well being. A rate in the neighborhood of 130 to 150 beats per minute suggests that labor is progressing satisfactorily. Heart rates that fall below 130 or rise above 150 suggest that problems may be brewing and that the fetus is experiencing distress. Figure 6–2 depicts the patterns of observer variation that occurred with different monitored fetal heart rates. When the true rate is within the 130 to 150 range, observer errors appear evenly scattered between overestimates and underestimates; but if monitored rates rise or fall to levels that indicate distress, the pattern of errors no longer appears symmetrically distributed. When the monitored rate drops below 130, observer errors tend to overestimate the rate, that is, bring it back toward the desirable range. When the rate exceeds 150, there is a tendency for observers to make estimates on the lower side of the electronic value.

This represents biased error. The cause for the bias is understandable; the hospital staff is not looking for trouble. The staff wants healthy deliveries and babies with good outcomes. Nevertheless, the message is clear. As with poor, giddy Troilus, expectation plays tricks on the mind. The wishes of the observer can influence measurements. Opportunities for measurement bias are abundant in medical studies and are one more problem that journal readers need to sniff out.

Investigator and Interviewer Bias

Measurement biases can be produced on both sides of the investigator/subject diad. For those who are collecting information for a study, the pitfalls are numerous. One's investment in the results or anticipation of how subjects are likely to respond can easily

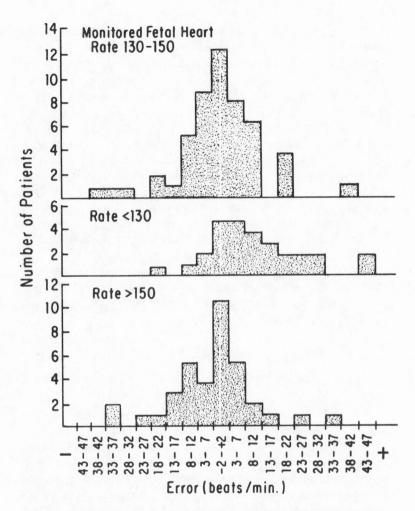

Figure 6-2. Error of auscultation of hospital staff at different fetal heart rates. (From Day, E. et al. [5] with permission.)

become a self-fulfilling prophecy. This is not to impugn the integrity of investigators. Objectivity is difficult to master. It is difficult for surgeons not to find benefits from their favorite operative procedures to alleviate hemorrhoids or for social workers looking for evidence of abuse and neglect not to uncover child maltreatment in a group known to be at high risk. It is unfair to expect an investigator trying a new antihypertensive agent to display total disinterest when taking the blood pressure of a subject under treatment. Even when investigators are not directly involved in data gathering, difficulties can occur. Choi and Comstock evaluated the effect that the personalities of hired interviewers had on subject responses to questionnaires in a community mental-health survey [2]. The instrument, administered by six different interviewers, measured a variety of mental-health characteristics, including sensitive items like troubles with alcohol, suicidal thoughts, nervous breakdowns, and stressful life events. In checking for observer variation, the authors noted that interviewer C produced subject scores that differed substantially from those of her colleagues. When the investigators attempted to identify items in the questionnaire that interviewers found embarrassing, Interviewer C reported feeling uncomfortable with questions pertaining to suicide, menstruation, marital happiness, and personal habits; none of the other five interviewers seemed disturbed by these topics. The authors concluded that a measurement bias was operating, that the personality and beliefs of the particular interviewer were systematically affecting responses on her questionnaires.

Subject Biases

Subjects can also introduce bias into the data-collection process. When subjects are invested in the experiment, have ideas about which therapy might be preferred, or simply want to please investigators by responding in a favorable way, results may be altered. We have seen the placebo effect in the study of myocardial revascularization for relief of angina pectoris, where patients' symptoms improved after sham operations. People responded from a need to feel relief and belief in the value of the treatment they were receiving. Patients who believe that a certain method of childbirth is beneficial are likely to report high satisfaction and favorable outcomes for their infants; parents of hyperactive children who have become convinced that food additives cause their child's aberrant behavior will see improvement in symptoms when these toxins are eliminated from the diet. Most patients want things to be better. They want to do things right! In fact, there is such a tendency for subjects to wish to respond in what they perceive of as a correct fashion that the term "social desirability bias" has been coined to describe the phenomenon.

This bias has been demonstrated in evaluations of health-education programs designed to encourage the use of car seats for young children. Pediatricians and other health professionals would love to find better ways of assuring the safe transport of infants and toddlers. Studies have evaluated a number of parent-education techniques including cautionary displays and pamphlets in the doctor's waiting room, staff demonstrations of the proper use of car seats, and physicians themselves counselling on the proper use of auto safety equipment. The success of the strategies, however, depends more on how measurements are made than on the educational method employed.

Two studies conducted on military populations acquired data in different ways and came up with disarmingly different results. In the first study parents of infants visiting a pediatric practice for a four-week check-up were allocated to receive one of four health-education strategies [13]. At the eight-week follow-up visit, these parents were questioned regarding their use of car seats. As can be seen from table 6–4, a small but tangible increase in proper restraint use appeared for families who received the health-education message from nurses or doctors. The evidence for this success, however, comes from parents' self-reports. Having been instructed by the practice to use car seats, parents were then quizzed about how well they obeyed instructions. This is fertile ground for producing a social desirability response bias.

Table 6–4   Reported Use of Acceptable Restraints for Infants Aged 8 Weeks in Passenger Automobiles after Various Parent-Education Strategies

Education Strategy (100 in each group)	Unsatisfactory Restraint	Satisfactory Restraint
None	91	9
Display	88	12
Pamphlet	92	8
Nurse	78	22
Physician	78	22

Adapted from Scherz, R. G. [13].

When another army officer looked at the same health-promotion problem, he assessed it in a different fashion [15]. Access to his base was limited through two gates, both guarded by members of the military police. He had the MPs record the restraint status of all children in automobiles passing through the gates. Then, for 18 months he diligently attempted to educate parents during well-baby visits and prenatal classes. The rate of car-seat use among children failed to improve when habits were again observed by the MPs. At the same time, parents "almost uniformly stated in the pediatric clinic that they (had) and (used) a safety seat."

Another source of consternation for investigators trying to observe subjects and collect data on them is the fact that the act of observation may change the behavior. This phenomenon goes under the fancy name of the "Hawthorne effect" (named not for a person but for a manufacturing plant where the effect was observed). The essence of the problem is that people may act differently when they know they are being watched. Examples of particular interest to clinicians come from projects that attempt to alter physician behavior, such as studies that try to improve the way doctors order laboratory tests or prescribe medications. Generally these efforts aim at educating physicians and stressing logical approaches to better decision-making. Any beneficial effects demonstrated in these experiments are probably more often due to the Hawthorne effect than to planned edification, however. Evidence to support this suspicion is found in the typical pattern that physician behavior follows in the wake of interventions. Inappropriate test ordering or prescribing generally decreases for a time, creating a satisfaction in the investigators that comes from watching rational enlightenment. Delight is usually short-lived, however. Given a few additional months, behavior reverts to its previous wayward level, suggesting that the transient improvement was related to the presence of the study rather than its message.

The report of an evaluation of an educational program to reduce ordering of thyroid function panels demonstrates this rebound phenomenon [12]. Here the authors attempted to influence physician-laboratory utilization during an educational conference in which doctors could characterize and analyze their motives for test ordering. In the three-month period following the conference, thyroid-panel ordering dropped (*see* figure 6–3). However, as time went on and clinicians forgot about the dark shadow of the inves-

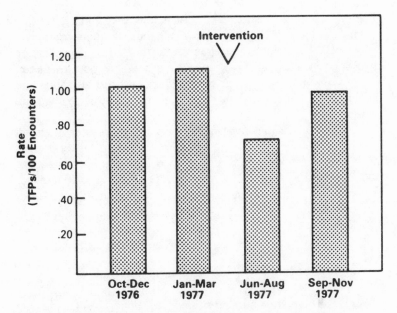

Figure 6-3. *Rate of ordering thyroid function panels (TFPs) by 3 month quarters. (From Rhyne, R. L. and Gehlbach, S. H. [12]. Reprinted with permission by Appleton-Century-Crofts.)*

tigators hovering over their shoulders, rates returned toward preintervention levels.

In the course of studies on practitioner/patient interactions, Starfield and colleagues found evidence that presence of an observer in the room with the doctor and patient changes the practitioner's recognition of patient problems [14]. When medical records completed after visits that were observed were compared with those of visits where no observer was present, a significantly higher percentage of patients' previous concerns were noted when the observer was in attendance.

Increasing comfort or familiarity with the measuring devices used to collect data may also affect subject response. It has been noted, for example, that patients having their blood pressures measured for the first time are much more likely to have elevated readings than after they have become acclimated to the medical setting. Studies that utilize pretests and post-tests to measure knowledge or repeat administrations of psychological inventories run the risk that a subject's earlier experience with the instrument will modify scores of subsequent administrations. Pretests may give learning clues or provide test-taking experience that make the post-test easier; subjects may remember their previous responses to questions in a psychological battery and be influenced by these when they are retested later.

All this means that investigators must be extremely cautious not to influence the course of human behavior in the process of observing it. For the reader, the lesson is to be on guard for biases introduced by the process of making measurements and to look for evidence that authors have taken steps to minimize the errors of data collection.

Controlling Measurement Error

There are a number of steps researchers can take to deal with the problems of unreliable and biased measurements. Some of them are already familiar. Keeping observers and subjects blind is probably the best known technique for reducing bias. In the so-called double-blind trial, neither the investigator nor the subject is allowed to become aware of which particular intervention is being used for any given subject. This approach is particularly suited for drug trials where identical pink and brown capsules can be concocted to contain the placebo and the active drug. There are some obvious limitations. It is very difficult, for example, to conceal the queen-sized bed and rococo decor of a birthing room from either physicians or patients. On the other hand, heroic efforts, such as the sham operations performed in the internal mammary ligation study, indicate the importance many investigators attach to the elimination of subject bias. Sometimes even the noblest of attempts falls short. In one study testing the efficacy of vitamin C in preventing the common cold, investigators took the necessary precaution of creating look-alike, unlabeled capsules and allocated them in random fashion to participants [8]. Since the therapeutic benefits of vitamin C have generated rather heated debate and the potential for subject and investigator bias was great, maintaining a double-blind design was particularly important. Unfortunately, savvy subjects foiled the system. Most of the volunteers in the study were employed at the National Institutes of

Health, and being a clever lot, they tasted capsule contents and detected the pills that contained ascorbic acid. With the code broken all bets against unbiased symptom reporting were off.

When measurements are made on interventions where investigators cannot maintain ignorance of the allocation, independent observers from the outside should be brought in. In the Leboyer childbirth study mentioned in chapter 5, for example, outcome assessments of neonates were made by observers who were kept scrupulously unaware of the method of childbirth used to bring the baby into the world [11].

There are other techniques for improving measurement reliability and minimizing observer error. These include:

1. *Establishing unambiguous standards.* When all observers are clear exactly how measurements are to be made, variability is reduced. Agreement on what size blood-pressure cuff should be used for which size arm and whether the fourth or fifth Korotokoff sound should be used as the diastolic estimate will produce more-reliable blood-pressure measurements. Deciding in advance how many millimeters an ST segment must be elevated to be compatible with an infarction pattern on an electrocardiogram will improve the consistency of the diagnosis of heart attack.

2. *Providing observers with supervised training and practice.* Once the guidelines for measurements have been established, observers need to practice their interviewing skills or measuring techniques to see where variances or biases are likely to occur. Medalie et al. have shown that poor interobserver agreement can be improved through training [10]. In their report from the Israel Ischemic Heart Disease project they demonstrated improved reliability in eliciting the history of chest pain and reduced the variance in sequential blood-pressure readings by focused retraining of physician examiners.

3. *Using multiple observers.* Although we have recognized the problems that multiple observers have agreeing with one another, several opinions are usually better than one. It is good form, for example, when diagnostic studies, such as x-rays or pathology specimens, are involved in results, to send these bits of data to independent observers for a second opinion. Even projects that rely on data acquired through seemingly straightforward methods such as chart audits, are better served when information is checked by more than one observer. Knowledgeable researchers will assess interrater reliability and supply readers with estimates of how closely different

raters agreed. The information is usually offered in terms of percent agreement or a coefficient of correlation, with the higher the agreement the better the reliability.

4. *Avoiding too many observers.* While corroboration of measurements is desirable, involving too many raters is asking for trouble. The quality of the broth is bound to suffer when the number of cooks exceeds limits of training and supervision.

While there are few guarantees that a research article is free from measurement error, readers may derive some comfort from evidence that an author has been rigorous in the pursuit of objective data. As with investigators who demonstrate cognizance of study-design problems such as attrition and allocation bias, authors who set forth the methods they use to guard against measurement error are more likely to gain our confidence.

Summary

When measurements are made, errors will occur. Pay particular attention to whether authors have:

1. Attempted to improve reliability by (a) establishing unambiguous measurement standards, (b) utilizing trained observers, and (c) corroborating observations with second opinions.

2. Taken steps to guard against biased measurement. Where possible, are both subjects and investigators blind to subject allocation? If the identity of treatments cannot be concealed, are attempts made to incorporate independent observers who are unaware of study hypotheses or treatment allocations?

References

1. BIRKELO, C. E., CHAMBERLAIN, W. E., PHELPS, P. S., SCHOOLS, P. E., ZACKS, D., AND YERUSHALMY, J. Tuberculosis case finding. A comparison of the effectiveness of various roentgenographic and photofluorographic methods. *JAMA* 133:359–365, 1947.

2. CHOI, I. AND COMSTOCK, G. W. Interviewer effect on responses to a questionnaire relating to mood. *Am. J. Epidemiol.* 101:84–92, 1975.

3. COCHRANE, A. L., CHAPMAN, P. J., AND OLDHAM, P. D. Observers' errors in taking medical histories. *Lancet* 1:1007–1009, 1951.

4. DAVIES, L. G. Observer variation in reports on electrocardiograms. *Br. Heart J.* 18:568, 1956.

5. DAY, E., MADDERN, L., AND WOOD, C. Auscultation of foetal heart rate: An assessment of its error and significance. *Br. Med. J.* 4:422–424, 1968.

6. DERRYBERRY, M. Reliability of medical judgments on malnutrition. *Public Health Rep.* 53:263–268, 1938.

7. DETRE, K. M., WRIGHT, E., MURPHY, M. L., AND TAKARO, T. Observer agreement in evaluating coronary angiograms. *Circulation* 52:979–986, 1975.

8. KARLOWSKI, T. R., CHALMERS, T. C., FRENKEL, L. D., KAPIKIAN, A. Z., THOMAS, L. L., AND LYNCH, J. M. Ascorbic acid for the common cold: A prophylactic and therapeutic trial. *JAMA* 231:1038–1042, 1975.

9. MEADE, T. W., GARDNER, M. J., CANNON, P., AND RICHARDSON, P. C. Observer variability in recording the peripheral pulses. *Br. Heart J.* 30:661–665, 1968.

10. MEDALIE, J. H., RISS, E., NEUFELD, H. N., ET AL. Some practical problems of observer variation in a large survey. In M. Eliakim and H. N. Neufeld (Eds.) *Cardiology—Current Topics and Progress.* New York and London: Academic Press, 1970.

11. NELSON, N. M., ENKIN, M. W., SAIGAL, S., BENNETT, K. J., MILNER, R., AND SACKETT, D. L. A randomized clinical trial of the Leboyer approach to childbirth. *N. Engl. J. Med.* 302:655–660, 1980.

12. RHYNE, R. L. AND GEHLBACH, S. H. Effects of educational feedback strategy on physician utilization of thyroid function panels. *J. Fam. Pract.* 8:1003–1007, 1979.

13. SCHERZ, R. G. Restraint systems for the prevention of injury to children in automobile accidents. *Am. J. Public Health* 66:451–456, 1976.

14. STARFIELD, B., STEINWACHS, D., MORRIS, J., BAUSE, G., SIEBERT, S., AND WESTIN, C. Presence of observers at patient-practitioner interactions: Impact on coordination of care and methodologic implications. *Am. J. Public Health* 69:1021–1025, 1979.

15. WALSH, M. J. Physician involvement in safety programs is not enough. *Pediatrics* 61:142, 1978.

SEVEN

Interpretation: Distributions, Averages, and the Normal

An obese statistician named Rouse
To his physician would continually grouse
"My head and feet are so little
And I bulge in the middle."
Said the doc, "You're quite 'normal', by Gauss."

A normal, red-blooded American boy is regarded as the ideal, but weather that is normal for the time of year is just the usual. The average physician is a standard representative of the breed; an average student is a bit dull. It is normal for a two-year-old child to engage in thumb sucking because it is typical behavior; a normal electrocardiogram is free of disease. The average score on a bio-chemistry examination is the mathematical midpoint; the statistical patterns of weights and heights collected on a group of college freshmen are noted to be normal distributions. Not since chapter 2 have we run up against such challenging semantics! But where the terminology for study designs was burdened by many terms that described a handful of concepts, we now find a variety of meanings attached to several words. The confusion arises when we begin to describe and interpret the data generated in medical studies. In this chapter we will examine ways in which techniques used to summarize data get misapplied and the confused interpretation that can result.

Frequency Distributions

Whenever we begin accumulating data, whether blood-pressure measurements from a community-screening program, the hemoglobin values of women in a prenatal clinic, or the National Board scores of third-year medical students, there is a need to organize our findings. One effective way of summarizing data is to create a frequency distribution, which is a map that depicts the number of times individual hemoglobin levels or board scores are found within the population being sampled.

Frequency distributions come in a variety of shapes and sizes. The most notorious was made famous by a gentleman named Gauss, a German mathematician who lived in the early nineteenth century. Gauss put forth the "law of errors," which stated that repeated measurements made on the same physical object fell in a predictable pattern or distribution that had certain mathematical properties and predictive features. Plots of Gaussian or normal distributions form a bell-shaped curve, a lovely symmetrical affair with a rounded peak in the middle and gracefully descending sides that approach but never quite reach zero (see figure 7–1a). Repeated measurements of the length of a table will show slight variations about the true value; readings close to the actual length will cluster toward the middle of the distribution and occur with relatively high frequency, while larger variations from the true length will be less common and distribute themselves toward both ends of the curve. Well enough! However, it was not long before Gauss' law had been borrowed and applied to the grouping of measurements made on different objects. The presumption was that if multiple measurements of a single individual's height were found to form a bell-shaped distribution, the heights of different individuals within a large group might just fall into a similar pattern. Over the years, the convenience of this assumption that biologic variation occurs in a Gaussian or normal pattern has swept aside the niggling warnings of purists that the assumption is incorrect. Elveback and colleagues plotted the fre-

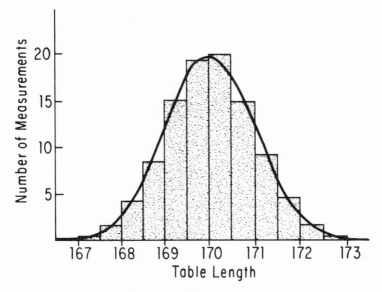

Figure 7–1a. *Normal distribution. Repeated measurements of a table's length.*

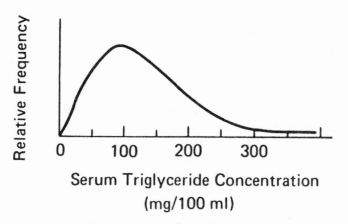

Figure 7–1b. *Skewed distribution. Serum triglyceride levels. (From Leaverton, P. E. A Review of Biostatistics: A Program for Self-Instruction. Boston: Little, Brown and Company, 1978, reprinted with permission. Copyright © 1978, Little, Brown and Company.)*

quency distributions of a number of common laboratory tests and found they varied from the Gaussian, mathematical approximations [2]. In general, the actual patterns of the biological measurements formed skewed distributions, meaning that the curves were asymmetrical with one side of the curve extending out in an elongated fashion (see figure 7–1b). Despite outcries against this misappropriation of mathematical theory, the notion that the normal distribution is a good approximation of the frequency pattern of biological measurements has become entrenched in medical thinking and medical writing.

Measures of Central Tendency

To facilitate discussion about distributions, several summary descriptors are in common use. These are the attributes of central tendency and variability. These concepts are not new to most readers, but because some misunderstandings have occurred over the years, a bit of review and clarification is worthwhile. The data in most distributions tend to cluster or center about a certain point as they array themselves along a range of possible values. By far the most commonly used measure of central tendency is the arithmetic mean or what most people speak of as the average. The mean of a distribution is derived by summing the individual values and dividing by the total number of determinations in the sample. The mean is a useful measure for conveying a general idea of where a population stands with respect to a given measure. If the women in a prenatal clinic have a mean hemoglobin of 8.6 grams, more concern about nutritional status might be raised than if the mean were 12.0 grams. A mean score of 70 by a medical-school class on the anatomy section of the National Board examinations could prompt a detailed look at the school's curriculum if the national average were 87 points. An average pulse rate of 54 beats per minute for a group of men completing a cardiac rehabilitation program suggests a conditioning effect when compared to a baseline mean pulse rate of 78. Less familiar but also useful as indicators of central tendency are the median and the mode. The median of a distribution is a midpoint at which one-half the observations fall below and one-half above the value. The mode is the most frequently encountered measurement in the distribution.

In bell-shaped, Gaussian distributions, the mean, the median, and the mode all land at precisely the same location, so that any of the three descriptors offers the same view of central tendency. However, as distributions become skewed, the three characteristics can be located at different points along the curve (*see* figure 7–2), and it becomes a matter of some debate as to which most fairly represents the distribution.

As an illustration, recall the study on the natural history of bacteriuria in schoolgirls [5]. This report described the long-term follow-up of a cohort of schoolgirls who were found to have asymptomatic urinary-tract infections during a school screening program. Figure 7–3 shows the frequency distribution of reinfections experienced by these subjects compared with the recurrence rate for the group of girls who served as controls. The distribution is markedly skewed. It shows that while most girls experienced relatively few reinfections, 20 percent of the cases had recurrences numbering five or more. The mean number of reinfections was between two and three, but this was not the usual experience. Most girls (the mode) did not have any, and the midway point of distribution (the median), where one-half had more and one-half had less, is one. The arithmetic mean of a distribution like this one is quite misleading.

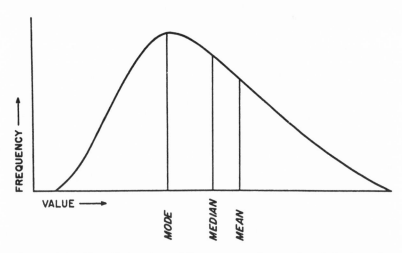

Figure 7–2. *Variable locations of the mean, median, and mode in skewed frequency distributions. (From Miale, J. B.* Laboratory Medicine: Hematology. *St. Louis: The C. V. Mosby Co., 1972. Reprinted with permission.)*

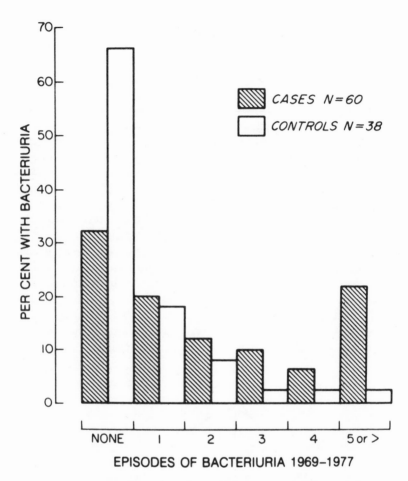

Figure 7-3. Episodes of bacteriuria in schoolgirls during follow-up studies of those showing the condition in screening programs. (From Gillenwater, J. Y. et al. [5]. Reprinted by permission of the New England Journal of Medicine, 301:397, 1979.)

Indicators of Variability

Estimates of the centers of distributions do not tell us all we need to know about arrays of data. It's also important to have a sense of whether measurements group about a central point or are widely spread. Do cholesterol values or anxiety scores of our study population all cluster together or do they scatter? If we are making repeated measurements on the same subject, as Gauss originally suggested, a distribution that hovers tightly about the mean suggests good measurement reliability. If we are measuring different individuals in a population, little variability suggests homogeneity among study subjects. Several estimators of variability are commonly employed. The range simply identifies extreme limits of a distribution. The weights of subjects in the experimental diet program ranged from 248 (the lowest) to 352 (the highest) pounds. Another guide to variability is the standard deviation. The standard deviation is calculated from a formula that sums the squares of differences between the group mean and each individual value. The greater these differences, the more spread the distribution and the larger the standard deviation. The notation commonly seen is "mean ± S.D.," and reference is frequently made to values that are one or two standard deviations from the mean. Within the span of one standard deviation on either side of the mean, we may expect to find approximately 68 percent of the values in a normal, frequency distribution; within two standard deviations lie 95 percent of the observations, and three standard deviations on either side of the mean encompass 99 percent of the values in the distribution. Figure 7–4 depicts all this. It is a convenient way of describing variation, but as we will see, it has been subjected to some serious misappropriations.

A third way of looking at the variations of a distribution is to use percentiles. Just as the median is the 50th percentile of a collection of data, the 75th or 95th percentiles can be determined and indicate that a particular head circumference or serum creatinine level lies at a point where it is larger than 75 percent or 95 percent of the other values in the group. An advantage of dividing distributions into percentiles is that it may be legitimately accomplished without respect to the shape of the distribution. Unlike the interpretation of standard deviations, the percentile system does not rely on the assumption of an underlying normal distribution.

Estimates of variability are useful descriptors. They give a per-

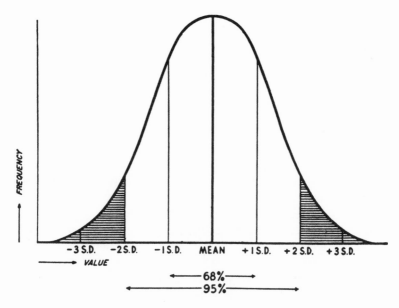

Figure 7-4. *Areas included within 1, 2, and 3 standard deviations (S.D.)
of the mean for normal distributions. (From Miale, J. B.* Laboratory Medicine: Hematology. *St. Louis: The C. V. Mosby Co., 1972. Reprinted with
permission.)*

spective that means or medians alone cannot provide. Suppose you
are attempting to decide on the therapeutic efficacy of cephalexin for
treatment of lymphadenitis due to *Staphylococcus.* You learn that
the blood level of drug needed to eradicate all the strains of
Staphylococcus aureus that lurk in your neighborhood is about $12\mu g$
of drug per 1 ml of serum. You find a report that offers the graphic
information depicted in figure 7–5a [1]. This chart shows the mean
serum levels of cephalexin at various time intervals following administration of a standard dose of the drug. It is easy to see from the curve
that the peak levels of the drug exceed the concentrations required
for eradication of the bacteria. It is also easy to forget that the graph
depicts only the mean or average levels achieved in the experiment.
When information on the variability of drug levels is included, as in
figure 7–5b, important information is added. With the bars depicting
the range on either side of the mean, it becomes apparent that there
is enough variability in absorption of the drug that the level of 12 μg

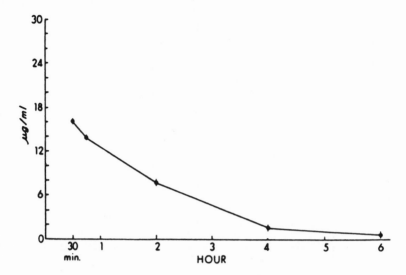

Figure 7–5a. *Mean serum levels of cephalexin following an oral dose.*

Figure 7–5b. *Mean and range of serum cephalexin levels following an oral dose (range indicated by vertical lines). (From Barton, L. L. and Feigin, R. P. [1]. Reprinted with permission.)*

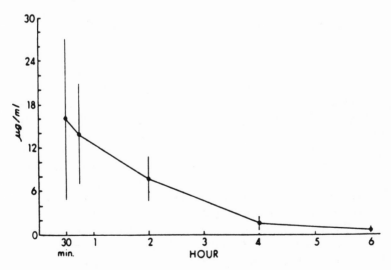

will not be reached some of the time. Summarizing data by use of the mean alone without some indications of variability can be misleading.

Normality

If averages are a potential point of confusion, major psychoses can result from trying to make sense of the ambiguous use of the term "normal." As suggested earlier, the word has taken on a number of meanings ranging from attributes that are typical or common to indicators of health to ideals to which we aspire. Murphy has written several papers on the subject and describes seven nuances of meaning for the term [6,7,8]. Feinstein [3] and Sackett [11] also offer discussions on the topic. By far, the biggest problem for clinicians comes from confusing the normal of statistical distributions with the presence or absence of disease. When Gauss defined his normal distribution, he certainly never dreamed that the phrases like "within normal limits" and "outside of the normal range" would become standard medical jargon.

Most clinicians appreciate the fact that the boundaries of illness are not always clear, especially when we begin discussing problems such as anemia, high blood pressure, or obesity. Does a hemoglobin of 10.5 grams signify ill health? Will a diastolic pressure of 90 mm lead to early death? Is 200 pounds too much for a 6'1" man to weigh? In our passion to distinguish between health and disease we have allowed ourselves to pretend that statistical distributions offer a measure of truth that they have not the power to provide. We plot the distribution of hemoglobin values for a group of pregnant women, determine the mean and two standard deviations, and decide that anyone whose level falls outside the area that encompasses 95 percent of hemoglobins is abnormal. We measure the serum potassium levels of our cardiac patients, sort the measurements, then announce that everyone with a value below 95% of the readings is suffering from the problem of hypokalemia. It is easy to see how the trap gets baited since we know that a great percentage of people who have anemia or who develop symptoms of potassium deficiency, will have hemoglobin or potassium values at the lower extremes of the respective distributions. But arbitrarily assigning subjects a disease without considering the clinical features of the disease or characteristics of the population being considered makes no sense. Such reasoning enables us to argue that the heaviest five percent of patients with anorexia nervosa are, in fact, overweight. To allow a cut point in a statistical distribution to define a disease is decidedly bad form.

Unfortunately, such indiscretions are not uncommon. A cross-sectional study was reported not long ago that set as its task defining the prevalence of hypertension in an adolescent population [4]. The design was straightforward. A group of over 10,000 eighth-grade students in a large school district had their blood pressures recorded by a special health-screening team. Wary of the problems of measuring blood pressure accurately, the investigators added some nice touches to minimize observer error. Members of the screening team underwent special training and were periodically monitored for reliability. Measurements were taken with a random zero mercury manometer, a device especially designed to reduce potential observer bias. Students were even allowed to sit quietly for 4 minutes before their pressures were obtained to minimize the effects of anxiety and activity. A very sound beginning that unfortunately was not sustained.

Once all 10,000 blood-pressure measures were obtained, they were arranged in a giant distribution and divided into percentiles. Then with a pronouncement that resounds with plausibility, the authors announce that about 9 percent of the adolescents screened had either systolic, diastolic, or both systolic and diastolic pressures above the 95th percentile. The conclusion is that these children are abnormal, that they have evidence of hypertension. Surprising results? Not exactly. It is a perfect circle of reasoning. If you create distributions of measurements, divide them into percentiles, and then define as diseased the upper 5 percent of systolic pressures and the upper 5 percent of diastolic pressures, it is easy to make a pretty good guess what the prevalence of hypertension is likely to be—about 5 percent for each group. In point of fact, there is no reason to suspect that any of these children has hypertension. The 95th percentile levels for systolic and diastolic pressure found from this initial screening were about 130 mm and 75 mm, respectively. These values are well below levels of adult blood pressure, that begin to correlate with the disease manifestations of hypertension. In the final analysis, none of the 10,000 subjects had a sustained diastolic pressure of 90 mm or more. Statistical distributions simply cannot be used to identify disease. The madness of this method is perhaps more dramatically illustrated by the use of normal distributions and standard deviations to define normal ranges of laboratory tests. Here the goal seems admirable enough—to provide clinicians with guidelines for interpreting laboratory data. Subtle mischief is afoot, however. When the clinician receives a report offering information that a patient's serum uric acid, bilirubin, or cholesterol level is outside the normal range, how does the news get processed? What does it mean? Usually physicians translate "outside normal limits" to mean "abnormal;" abnormal means "unhealthy" and unhealthy means "diseased." The syllogism is not totally unreasonable. After all, we know that people who have gout suffer from high uric-acid levels, that liver disease is characterized by abnormally high bilirubin concentrations, and that increased levels of cholesterol in the blood are associated with coronary artery disease.

The question is, how closely associated with disease are these abnormal chemistries? The answer requires knowing how the laboratory folks who produce these normal limits go about their business. Just what constitutes a normal range, and what sort of population sample is used to determine normality? It is rarely evident from the laboratory reports, but typically, normal limits are concocted by the old standard-deviation routine. Uric acid or bilirubin determinations are performed on a large sample of blood specimens, a distribution is constructed, and the area that contains 95% of the values is blocked off to represent normality. Are values that lie outside this hallowed zone really abnormal? Do they represent disease? That depends upon who the reference subjects are. If the technicians, custodians, and administrators that work at the laboratory comprise the sample, or volunteers from the local college or nursing school, it is likely that few, if any, of them have gout or obstructive liver disease. They are all healthy, yet by selecting the extremes of the distribution, 5 percent are automatically identified as abnormal or diseased. As with the adolescent hypertensives, its an exercise in logical tail-chasing. There are also some interesting economic implications.

In an age of poly-laboratory, commercial biochemical laboratories have made financial hay out of semantic confusion. By providing useful, normal values to aid interpretation of test results, they have created profit from uncertainty. If a population of healthy adults is used to determine the distribution of uric acid or cholesterol values, and the two standard deviation cut-off points are used, 5 percent of nondiseased subjects will have values categorized as abnormal. With automation, multiple determinations are possible on a single blood sample at little increase in cost over a single test. However, when 5 percent of each of 20 biochemical determinations is routinely classified as deviant, the likelihood that any nondiseased individual will have all 20 determinations reported as normal is only 36 percent. The probability that each test will be normal is 0.95; that of test A being normal and test B being normal . . . and test T being normal is $0.95 \times 0.95 \ldots \times 0.95$. For 20 tests that is 0.95^{20} or, 0.36. Clinicians who order multitest panels on patients must either ignore frequently occurring abnormal values or repeat the test in hopes that aberrant values will return to the normal range. Repeating the panels creates the potential for further classification errors, more confusion and adds substantially to the medical bill. Sackett has discussed this problem and summarizes the situation quite nicely [11]:

> The use of a statistical concept such as the standard deviation to set the limits of normal for clinical laboratory tests represents the cross-sterilization of disciplines, for it represents taking a misunderstood concept from sampling statistical theory and misapplying it in an individual clinical situation.

A final morsel for the normal stew, entitled "Microcephaly in a Normal School Population" [12], presents the spectrum of confusion that surrounds normality. The author of this paper sets as the major objective for his study, "to examine the prevalence of microcephaly, defined as a head circumference greater or equal to two standard deviations below the mean in a normal school population." We are off to quite a start. Microcephaly, while literally meaning the condition of having a small head, has connotations of abnormality, that is, of being associated with mental retardation. That is the only reason it is worthy of concern. The prevalence of microcephaly in a normal school population tastes of the non sequitur—normal in this case suggesting without disease or mental handicap.

The author gathers a group of approximately 1,000 students aged 5 to 18 years, who are attending regular classes in a suburban school district. Head circumferences of these youngsters are measured and compared against a standard to determine the frequency of microcephaly. Nineteen children, or 1.9 percent of the population, fall into this abnormal group. The author remarks,

> . . . the finding of 1.9 percent prevalence of microcephaly in a normal school population was not unexpected, since the author anticipated that there would be a significant number of children with microcephaly and normal intelligence enrolled in regular classrooms.

He is certainly correct in his expectation. Finding a 1.9 percent prevalence of microcephaly, when microcephaly is defined as the lower 2 percent of a frequency distribution, should not be unanticipated. It is a given. Examining the reference standard used in classifying children, we find the standard was derived in exactly the same manner as the experimental data were obtained, by measuring the head circumferences of a large number of presumably healthy children [9]. The author reaches the dramatic conclusion that "although head-circumference measurement remains a valuable clinical tool, a head-circumference measurement greater than two standard deviations below the mean is not uniformly associated with mental retardation." We cannot help but agree with him since, as he also points out, "our population was selected from children attending regular classrooms (and) mentally retarded children with microcephaly would not be included in the study population." The study is an exercise in confused logic and imprecise usage—interchanging concepts of "usual" and "healthy" with arbitrary cut points in statistical distributions.

Regression to the Mean

There is one last bit of business about interpreting distributions that readers should master. It has to do with an impressive sounding phenomenon called regression to the mean. Regression can occur any time investigators classify subjects according to measurements that lie at the extremes of a distribution and then remeasure them. On average, the repeat values will appear less extreme, that is, they will regress toward the mean of the total population. Studies describing hypertension detection and treatment programs are at substantial risk of demonstrating this regression phenomenon. Typically, a group of shopping-center browsers submit to having their blood pressures taken. These pressure determinations form a frequency distribution with a mean of perhaps 120/80. At the upper end of the distribution are a number of people whose diastolic pressures exceed 90 mm. These people are labelled hypertensive and are the individuals on whom follow-up and treatment attention will be lavished. They are offered pills, weight-control programs, relaxation training, or biofeedback, and a gratifying response is found. At follow-up, the average diastolic pressure of the group has fallen. It is concluded that therapy has been successful. While some of this improvement may be due to treatment, part of it is inevitably due to regression.

Remembering from chapter 6 about the unavoidable variability of measurements, we should recognize that classification errors will occur in a one-shot screening attempt. Given the combined effects of the physiologic variation of individual blood pressures and measurement error, misclassifications are bound to occur. If we use 90 mm as our dividing line for designating hypertension, there will be people whose true diastolic pressure is 89 mm but who measure 96 mm on the occasion of the screening. These people will get misclassified as hypertensive. Of course, errors in classification occur in the other direction as well; a person whose true diastolic pressure is 95 mm may register 88 mm on screening day and become relegated to the nonhypertensive group. However, when we screen and establish a cutoff, we immediately lose interest in people who fall below the 90 mm mark; they never get measured again and remain incorrectly grouped. We only reassess people whose pressures are found to be high. Since some of them have been misclassified, subsequent blood-pressure determinations will tend to restore them to their rightful places as nonhypertensives. The result is that, on average, the group designated as having high blood pressure will have lower pressures the second time around. Figure 7–6 is a schematic representation of the problem.

The study that screened Texas eighth graders for high blood pressure demonstrated the regression effect quite nicely [4]. In the first round of blood-pressure measuring, nine percent of the adolescents had "high blood pressure." These young people were then re-examined on two occasions before a final figure of 1.6% was announced as the prevalence of hypertension. Since no treatment was involved in this program, there must be some other explanation for

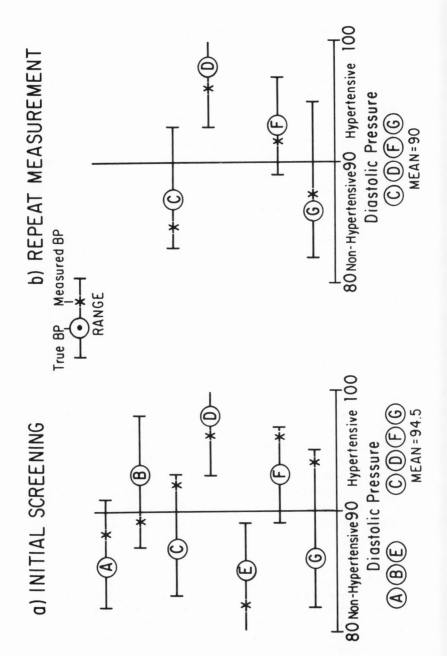

the normalizing of so many of the subjects who were classified as hypertensive initially.

In part, the reduction probably reflects decreased anxiety on the part of students as they became familiar with the measuring situation. Patients frequently display mild elevations in blood pressure on a first visit to the clinic, which disappears in subsequent visits. Regression to the mean is also operating. The key to this effect is the repeated measurement of only subjects initially classified as over the arbitrary cut point of the distribution; in this example, those with blood pressure above the 95th percentile.

Let us look at one more example. As part of a clinical trial evaluating the benefits of tonsillectomy in preventing recurrent throat infections, an informative natural history study was performed [10]. The authors set stringent criteria for entry into their controlled trial of operative procedures. Included were documentation of at least seven episodes of throat infection in the year prior to entry into the study, five episodes in each of the preceding two years, or three episodes in each of the three years prior to study. Of some 300 children evaluated, 95 had histories of recurrent throat infections that met the standards but lacked sufficient documentation for inclusion. Generally, this meant that parents reported the problem, but it was not confirmed by a physician or health worker. Sixty-five of these children were followed for a year to see what their natural history of subsequent throat infections would be. Results showed that only 11 of the 65 had a sufficient number of throat infections in the follow-up year to qualify for tonsillectomy. Overall the group had many fewer throat infections during the observation year than had been previously reported. This is a rather provocative finding since, for this group of children at least, an operation performed at the time of enrollment might well have been credited for the subsequent decline in throat infections. As it is, the authors attribute the findings to natural reduction in illness as children get older and a certain unrelia-

---

Figure 7–6.   *Regression to the mean in a blood pressure (BP) screening program. Measured pressures (x) in initial screening misclassify subjects C and G as hypertensive. Mean for "hypertensives" (C, D, F, G) is 94.5 mm. On repeat measurement C and G are closer to their true BPs (O). Mean for C, D, F, and G falls to 90 mm. B is misclassified as nonhypertensive but never has repeat measurement.*

bility in parents' estimates of past morbidity. Certainly problems with the changing natural history and observer bias are likely. However, there is also a regression effect. In this instance, children have been selected for study only if they have experienced a very high number of throat infections. They are out on the tail of the sore-throat-frequency distribution. Children who have been selected on the basis of seven episodes of throat infection in a single year are likely on statistical grounds alone to have fewer episodes in a subsequent year.

The regression effect can occur anytime clinical or laboratory measurements are made on groups of people, and individuals are selected for further study on the basis of cut points made on ends of a distribution. Readers need to be aware of this phenomenon since, as is illustrated by the hypertension and sore-throat examples, statistical regression can easily be interpreted as therapeutic benefit. An understanding of the problem suggests its remedy. Before a classification is made, multiple measurements should be obtained to gain a more reliable estimate of a person's true value. Knowledgeable investigators studying hypertension, for example, will take three or four pretreatment blood pressures to establish an estimate of the patient's true blood pressure before any classification or intervention is undertaken. When this precaution is not observed, let the reader beware!

Summary

The problems of making reliable and valid measurements are compounded when measurements are misrepresented or misinterpreted in frequency distributions. Questions of particular relevance for readers to ask are:

1. How are distributions of data summarized? Are distributions that are likely to be skewed assumed to be normal? When arithmetic means are employed to describe central tendency, do they summarize the data fairly? Are estimates of variability given when data are presented?

2. Are statistical distributions used to define clinical disease? When normal distributions become arbiters of health and disease, watch out! What is the health status of people on whom reference

distributions are created? Are any clinical features used to support arbitrary cut-offs as indicators of disease?

3. Is regression to the mean occurring? If extremes of frequency distributions are used to classify subjects, has care been taken to avoid misclassification? Will subsequent measurements tend to regress and spuriously suggest a treatment effect?

References

1. BARTON, L. L. AND FEIGIN, R. D. Childhood cervical lymphadenitis: A reappraisal. *J. Pediatr.* 84:846–852, 1974.

2. ELVEBACK, L. R., GUILLIER, C. L., AND KEATING, F. R., JR. Health, normality, and the ghost of Gauss. *JAMA* 211:69–75, 1970.

3. FEINSTEIN, A. R. *Clinical Biostatistics.* St. Louis: C. V. Mosby Co., 1977.

4. FIXLER, D. E., LAIRD, W. P., FITZGERALD, V., STEAD, S., AND ADAMS, R. Hypertension screening in schools: Results of the Dallas study. *Pediatrics* 63:32–36, 1979.

5. GILLENWATER, J. Y., HARRISON, R. B., AND KUNIN, C. M. Natural history of bacteriuria in schoolgirls. A long-term case-control study. *N. Engl. J. Med.* 301:396–399, 1979.

6. MURPHY, E. A. AND ABBEY, H. The normal range—a common misuse. *J. Chron. Dis.* 20:79–88, 1967.

7. MURPHY, E. A. The normal, and the perils of the sylleptic argument. *Perspect. Biol. Med.* 15:566–582, 1972.

8. MURPHY, E. A. The normal. *Am. J. Epidemiol.* 98:403–411, 1973.

9. NELLHAUS, G. Head circumference from birth to eighteen years. Practical composite international and interracial graphs. *Pediatrics* 41:106–114, 1968.

10. PARADISE, J. L., BLUESTONE, C. D., BACHMAN, R. Z., ET AL. History of recurrent sore throat as an indication for tonsillectomy. Predictive limitations of histories that are undocumented. *N. Engl. J. Med.* 298:409–413, 1978.

11. SACKETT, D. L. The usefulness of laboratory tests in health-screening programs. *Clin. Chem.* 19:366–372, 1973.

12. SELLS, C. J. Microcephaly in a normal school population. *Pediatrics* 59:262–265, 1977.

EIGHT

Interpretation: Statistical Significance

There are three kinds of lies: lies, damn lies, and statistics.
—Disraeli

Mr. Disraeli's discomfort with statistics is shared by many clinicians. Somehow the brief exposure to the biostatistics courses offered in college or medical school seems woefully inadequate. A working understanding of p-values, chi-squares and the null hypothesis is difficult to come by and easily lost. The current sophistication of statistical presentations in journal articles makes it tempting to abdicate responsibility for interpretations of statistical significance to the statisticians and editors, but that is probably not a wise plan.

For the most part, biostatistics and clinical research work well together. Statistical-significance testing keeps overly optimistic clinical anecdotes in a proper perspective, but there are instances where the fit is not good, and the clinical message of the study is drowned in a statistical flood. In this chapter, we will explore the principles underlying the use of tests of statistical significance, clarify some statistical terminology, and look at some common, subtle (and usually unintentional) statistical traps that await the unwary reader.

Inference

To understand statistical significance we need to know about making inferences. An inference is a generalization made about a large group or population from the study of a sample of that population. To illustrate, suppose you have just completed Saturday morning house calls and stopped by Pritchard's country store to take in a Dr. Pepper and some rural wisdom. Behind the flour sack on which you perch are two apple barrels: one holds red Jonathans, the other, Golden Delicious (to which you are partial). Unfortunately, there has been some mixing of the two varieties so the red-apple barrel has some goldens in it and vice versa. Proprietor Pritchard, always keen for a wager, says he will give you your favorite if you correctly identify the red-apple and golden-apple barrels by examining only five apples. You reach back, extract the apples from one of the barrels, and finding one is red and four are yellow announce that you have found the golden-apple barrel.

You've just made an inferential statement, that is, a judgment about a characteristic of a population (the composition of a whole barrel of apples) from evaluating a sample of the population (five apples). Simple enough. However, there is a chance that you are wrong. The proportions of your sample may not reflect the composition of the entire barrel. You may have chanced to pick the only four yellow apples in the entire red-apple barrel, made an incorrect inference, and lost the bet. To reduce the likelihood of making an error your best strategy would be to enlarge the size of your sample. Instead of 5 apples, you could examine 20; or you could increase your sample to 50 or 100 apples. As you come closer to counting the entire barrel of apples your chance of making a mistaken inference decreases. If, finally, you study all the apples, you are no longer making an inference, and you can be certain of the composition of the barrel.

Most medical studies, whether testing the efficacy of steroids in treating poison ivy or looking for an association between exposure to asbestos and occurrence of lung tumors, evaluate samples of larger populations. We examine 50 patients, 200 workers in a single industrial plant, or even an entire community, hoping to generalize about all patients, all chemical plants, or society at large; and as with picking apples at the country store, there is a chance we will be misled by our sample.

Sampling Variability

Let us suppose we are interested in testing the claim that the antibiotic, amoxicillin, causes less diarrhea than its cousin, ampicillin. We begin by giving amoxicillin to 50 patients in our practice. We ask the patients to report any episodes of diarrhea that occur while they are taking the medication. It turns out that six patients (12 percent) report diarrhea. So far, so good. We would like to be able to predict the behavior of all patients who receive amoxicillin. To verify our earlier results, we select another sample of 50 patients and repeat the experiment. This time only 8 percent of patients experience the side effect. Repeating the experiment yet a third time reveals an incidence of diarrhea of 10 percent.

In attempting to delineate the true incidence of diarrhea for all patients who receive the drug, making inferences from samples of 50, we have uncovered the problem of sampling variability. Each estimate we gather is at slight variance from its predecessor. If we continue repeating our samples of 50 patients, we will find that our collection of results begins to form a pattern. Values begin to cluster around certain recurrent percentages. The results group around 10%, which is not only the most common result (the mode) but is located in the center of the distribution (the median). We find some estimates both higher and lower than 10 percent, but these become less frequent as they become more extreme.

If we had nothing better to do than continue taking our samples of 50 patients over and over, we would form a sampling distribution for the incidence of diarrhea among people given amoxicillin. Figure 8–1 illustrates what this distribution might look like. The conclusion we make from examining the distribution is that the true incidence of this side effect is 10 percent with the understanding that any estimate we make from a single sample of 50 patients may be slightly off the mark. We can examine the plot of diarrhea frequencies and estimate how often we would find a rate as high as 16 percent or as low as 4 percent. Assuming our experiments are performed reliably, we can predict this will occur relatively infrequently—about 1 in 20 times.

We still have not answered the question of whether amoxicillin has a lower frequency of diarrhea than ampicillin. Let us find another group of 50 patients, subject them to ampicillin, and ask for reports of diarrhea. The patients provide us with the information that 16

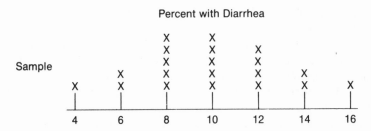

Figure 8-1. *Percent of patients receiving amoxicillin who develop diarrhea. Based on samples of 50 patients each.*

percent of them encountered the side effect. That is an apparent increase over the 10 percent figure we calculated for amoxicillin, but we did note that, occasionally, sampling variability would produce an estimate as high as 16 percent for the frequency of amoxicillin-induced diarrhea. Does the rate we have found for our single sample of ampicillin patients represent a true difference from amoxicillin or have we drawn the 1 in 20 sample from the high end of the same distribution?

The Null Hypothesis and Statistical Significance

At this point we need to bring in a major nemesis—the null hypothesis. Lack of understanding of just how the null hypothesis operates is the cause of countless headaches. It is different from a research hypothesis. The proposition that amoxicillin causes less diarrhea than ampicillin is a research hypothesis. We expect that by comparing the two drugs, we will find a difference in the incidence of this side effect. The null hypothesis states that the drugs are not different. It is strictly a statistical convention, used for helping us decide how likely it is that our results have been produced by quirks of sampling.

Testing for statistical significance using the null hypothesis has been likened to the judicial process of assuming innocence until proven guilty. We make the assumption (contrary to our research

hypothesis) that the true incidence of diarrhea for the two preparations is no different: ampicillin is innocent of higher diarrhea. Taking on the role of prosecuting attorney, we then try to demonstrate
beyond reasonable doubt that in fact there is a difference. Rejecting
the null hypothesis supports the research hypothesis.

We know that repeating the amoxicillin experiment on 50
people would yield a result of 16 percent incidence of diarrhea only 1
in 20 times. That is a reasonably unlikely occurrence. So when we
learn that ampicillin causes diarrhea in 16 percent of patients in our
single sample, we have useful evidence to argue. We can say that if
ampicillin really behaved like amoxicillin, it would be unlikely (a 5
percent chance) that we would find a 16 percent rate of diarrhea in a
single sample. We reject the null hypothesis on that basis, proclaim
the drugs have different rates of diarrhea, and rest our case. Unfortunately, we are left with the nagging thought that we may have made
a mistake. There is, after all, a 1 in 20 chance that the drugs behave
no differently and that we unwittingly sampled from that far end of
the distribution.

That is the risk we take any time we make a statistical inference
and a pronouncement of statistical significance. We are saying that
we think ampicillin and amoxicillin produce dissimilar rates of
diarrhea but that there is a 5 percent chance that we are wrong. This
mistake is referred to as the alpha error, or type I error, and the
likelihood of making it, the p-value. The p-value is the probability
that we are rejecting the null hypothesis and saying that the rates of
diarrhea are being estimated from two different populations (of drug
side effects) when, in fact, we are sampling different parts of a single distribution.

Most often, results of clinical studies are said to be statistically
significant, that is unlikely to be due to chance, if the p-value is less
than 5 percent (.05) or 1 percent (.01). But there is nothing magical
about these levels of probability. The .05 tradition began in the
1920s with an influential statistician named Fisher. It has been habit
ever since. Frequently we read articles in which a wide variety of
p-values is used, ranging from .05 to values that are many times
smaller. Small p-values like .001 or .0001 are important to the extent
that they tell us that differences we observe are unlikely to be mistakes in inference due to sampling, but we need to be wary of a
subtle illusion that is created by these impressive numbers.

Some Problems of Statistical Significance

The size of the p-value does not indicate the importance of the result. It is tempting to believe that very small p-values indicate great discoveries. Terms such as "highly significant results" and "very highly significant results" are liberally sprinkled through journals. Consider an article that demonstrated a correlation between alcohol consumption and elevated blood pressure [6]. In this study, daily intake of alcoholic beverages was compared with blood pressure readings for patients in a prepaid group practice. A difference in average blood pressure was found between individuals who drank small amounts of alcohol and those with high intake. Those who drank more had higher blood pressure. This finding was reported as statistically significant, with a p-value of 10^{-24}. Extraordinary! Enough "highlys" in that significant result to cover an entire page. But what does this value really mean? Simply that the difference found is not likely to have occurred because of sampling alone. It does not mean that the findings are of major medical importance, nor does it mean that alcohol consumption is a major cause of hypertension. It means only that chance is an unlikely explanation for the results. This extremely small p-value is due to the size of the sample, 80,000 people in all. Very large samples become close approximations of the populations they are estimating, so any differences that are found are likely to be real (like examining all the apples in the barrel). There is little reason to report such an absurd p-value. The results are scarcely more credible than had they been achieved with a 1 in 10,000 likelihood of making an erroneous conclusion. Yet, it is difficult for a reader not to be awed by such a statistical *tour de force*, even though it adds nothing of substance to the study.

Results may be statistically significant but clinically trivial. Just as it is easy to be impressed by small p-values, so can we be seduced into equating statistical significance with clinical importance. Consider a frequently referenced article on the therapy of otitis media [11]. In this clinical trial the authors compare the efficacy of several drugs commonly used in treating ear infections. Among the drugs tested was an antihistamine. In comparing the responses of patients prescribed the antihistamine with those not treated, a statistically significant reduction in treatment failures was found when the antihistamine was used. The results of the study are summarized in

Table 8–1   Failure Rates for Patients with Otitis Media Treated With and Without Antihistamines

	With Antihistamines	Without Antihistamines
Patients treated	250	264
Treatment failures	4 (1.6%)	13 (4.9%)

Based on Stickler, G. B., et al. [11] by permission of the American Medical Association. Copyright © 1967, The American Medical Association.

table 8–1. It is easy to conclude that antihistamines should be used in the treatment of otitis media. Let us examine these data more closely.

The number of children treated with the antihistamine was 250; the number left untreated, about the same. For the treated group, there was a failure rate of approximately 2 percent compared with a 5 percent rate for those left untreated. This two-fold difference in failure rates is indeed statistically significant; it would have occurred only 5 in 100 times by chance. The question remains, however, is the treatment clinically important? Among the 514 children who had ear infections, only 9 treatment failures were prevented by the use of the medication. Is this benefit dramatic enough to warrant large-scale deployment of antihistamines as a major weapon against otitis? Probably not. That is 57 prescriptions written for each failure averted. Again the hefty sample size magnifies a small difference between populations into a significant finding. The findings may be real but have little to add to clinical practice. While large samples can produce statistical differences that may be unimportant clinically, small sample sizes can cause an even more treacherous trap.

Differences that are not statistically significant are not necessarily unimportant.   We have already agreed that most medical researchers look for differences and that rejecting the null hypothesis "proves" the difference. However, failure to reject the null hypothesis does not guarantee that differences observed are not real, nor that the groups being compared are the same. Another study of otitis media illustrates the point.

Roddey et al. designed a clinical trial to test whether myringotomies aided the resolution of ear infections [10]. To a standard antibiotic regimen they randomly added the minor operative proce-

Table 8-2 Failure Rates for Patients with Otitis Media Treated With and Without Myringotomy

	With Myringotomy	Without Myringotomy
Patients treated	113	127
Treatment failures	27 (24%)	44 (35%)

Based on Roddey, O. F., Jr., et al. [10] by permission of the American Medical Association. Copyright © 1966, American Medical Association.

dure for one-half the patients. Among children having myringotomies a treatment failure rate of 24 percent was found, compared with 35 percent for those in whom the procedure was not performed (*see* table 8-2). The difference just missed statistical significance, at the chosen p of .05; for the number of children observed, quirks of sampling could produce the same difference between 5 percent and 10 percent of the time. That was not enough evidence for Roddey to win his case and reject the null hypothesis. The findings might be due to chance. These conclusions have been summarized in subsequent articles as demonstrating that "myringotomy made no difference in the resolution of otitis media." This is not really true. Roddey found a difference. In fact, myringotomy prevented more treatment failures (11 per 100 patients) than did the use of antihistamines (3 per 100 patients). Sample size is again the key. Had Roddey studied the same number of patients as were in the antihistamine trial and found the same 11 percentage points difference in failure rate, his results would have been statistically significant. As it is, we can only say that the fewer treatment failures found after myringotomy might have been an artifact of sampling. This leads to another type of error that occurs in hypothesis testing.

Beta Errors and Statistical Power

Two kinds of mistakes can be made in the search for statistical significance. The first occurs when we reject the null hypothesis, and it is true. We claim two treatments are dissimilar and, in fact, they are no different. This is the alpha, or type I, error we discussed with reference to ampicillin and amoxicillin. The second potential hypothesis-testing error is suggested in the myringotomy and otitis media example. Failing to reject the null hypothesis when it is not true is a beta, or type II, mistake. A true treatment effect or difference is being overlooked. Table 8–3 schematizes the correct and incorrect decisions that can be made when we are testing the null hypothesis. Rejecting the notion that two treatments are identical when they are different, and finding no difference when none exists are correct decisions. Of the incorrect conclusions, the alpha error is most familiar to clinicians. We worry about claiming a new treatment is effective when chance could have produced the difference we observe. We are accustomed to seeing p-values, and conceptualization of this first type of error is reasonably straightforward.

Coming to an understanding of beta errors is a bit trickier. We wish to avoid making the mistake of missing a therapeutic effect; that is, of accepting the idea that two treatments are the same simply because we cannot reject the null hypothesis and state they are different. But, once we start speaking of rejecting and accepting differences, the question becomes, "Differences of what size?" Roddey found an 11 percent difference in cure rate between his myringotomy group and controls. He might have observed a difference of 8, 2, or 16 percent. The range of possibilities is infinite. When we speak of the likelihood of missing a treatment effect in our hypothesis testing, the size of the difference we are looking for is crucial. For each possible difference that might exist, there is a different proba-

Table 8–3 Errors Encountered in Testing the Null Hypothesis to Evaluate Efficacy of Treatments A and B

		Null Hypothesis *(Treatment A = Treatment B)*	
		True (No difference)	**False** (Difference)
Decision (based on statistical test)	**Accept** (No difference)	Correct	Type II, beta error
	Reject (Difference)	Type I, alpha error	Correct

bility of making a beta error. The whole business of beta error is an interplay between the magnitude of difference, the number of subjects involved, and the alpha level at which experimenters decide they will reject the null hypothesis.

Researchers can lessen their chances of making beta errors by altering these three basic ingredients. We speak of the process of reducing beta error as improving experimental power. Statistical power is the complement of beta error (power = 1 − beta error); the lower the beta error, the greater the power. The power of an experiment is the likelihood that the experiment will detect a treatment effect of a particular size (a difference) for a particular number of experimental subjects. The higher the power, the better our chances of finding the treatment benefit, if it is there. The most obvious way of increasing power is to increase the number of subjects studied. If Roddey had studied twice the number of subjects and found the same 11 percent difference, it would have been statistically significant (occurred by chance less than 5 percent of the time). Power is also influenced by the size of the difference. For a given number of subjects, an experiment will have a higher probability of detecting a large treatment effect than a small difference. A 50 percent difference in cure rates for the original numbers of myringotomy and control subjects would have a high probability of rejecting the null hypothesis. Power may also be improved if we are willing to raise the alpha level. Roddey's findings would have been statistically significant at an alpha level of 10 percent. But to increase the likelihood of finding a statistically significant difference by changing alpha, we must also increase the possibility of falsely claiming an experimental effect. Comfort with these concepts requires some pondering, but they are worth trying to master. Several discussions of the topic are available [1,2].

Ideally, power calculations should be made before an experiment is performed. Investigators should decide on the number of subjects they require based on estimates of the size of difference they wish to detect and the certainty with which they desire to pinpoint that difference. In general, a power of 80 percent to 90 percent is considered respectable. However, things do not always work out that way.

Freiman and colleagues analyzed 71 studies from major medical journals that reported negative results, that is, no difference was found between treatments studied [2]. They found a high percentage of these studies could have missed an important difference in therapies because an inadequate number of subjects was evaluated. Many of the studies actually showed trends that suggested a treatment worked, but the authors concluded the therapy was no different from control simply because they could not reject the null hypothesis. Results reported in experimental and observational studies may be negative not because there are no differences but because the power of the study was too low to detect meaningful differences. Researchers should comment about power when they present negative results. They should provide some estimate of the probability that, for the number of subjects studied and the alpha level considered reasonable for rejecting the null hypothesis, a meaningful difference between groups would have been detected.

When estimates of power are not provided, two bits of common sense may help decide whether "no statistically significant difference" really means a negative result. First, the magnitude of the difference between groups can be assessed. If the average disastolic blood pressure in a group treated with a new antihypertensive medication is 93 mm and that of control patients is 94 mm, it seems unlikely that the treatment is going to offer an important clinical effect regardless of the size of the sample. Sometimes results actually favor the control or placebo. That makes it even less likely a real difference is being overlooked. Some note should also be made of the number of subjects in the study. Generalizing is chancy business, since sufficient sample size will vary with the size of difference being sought and the alpha level. Nonetheless, treatment groups of less than 50 subjects are often too small to demonstrate any but the more dramatic treatment effects. To be reasonably certain of finding a difference of 25 percent or less, groups must often be 100 or more.

Testing for Statistical Significance May Be Irrelevant

Bearing in mind that significance testing simply tells us the likelihood of finding results because of sampling variability, we can find examples of studies where chance is not really at issue. In a study of the effect of weight reduction on the blood pressure of overweight, hypertensive patients [9], information is presented comparing weight loss among dieting patients and a nondieting control group. Of 81 patients who were dieting every patient lost weight; the lowest loss reported was 3 kg and the average about 9 kg. The control group underwent very little change in weight, losing less than a kilogram on average. In assessing these findings the authors note, "this reduction was highly significant . . . p < .001." Of course, there is nothing really wrong with his statistical claim. However, the finding is so obvious it scarcely merits statistical enforcement. We do not need a p-value to tell us that patients who adhere to a diet and uniformly lose weight differ from nondieting controls.

Descriptive studies sometimes employ statistics that give an appearance of profundity while illustrating the obvious. In an article on prevention of injuries to children in automobiles [7], a series of 200 roadside observations was made of safety practices and their relationship to other "characteristics of the journey." A positive relationship was found between observing children riding in the rear seat (a good safety practice) and the number of adults riding in the automobile. This finding is reported as statistically significant at the p < .001 level. Impressive! But at second glance, it is hardly an insight likely to revolutionize highway safety. The percentage of children in the back seat rises as the number of adults in the automobile increases. Children have to sit somewhere, and since adults usually lay claim to the front seat, the kids get displaced to the back. Attaching a fancy p-value to trivial observations does little to enhance their importance.

Alternate Explanations of the Observed Difference

Having observed differences that are statistically significant, it is tempting to conclude that our treatments or theories are responsible for observed effects. Unfortunately, this may not be true. Remember, rejecting the null hypothesis is only a guide to the role chance may have played in creating differences.

Capricious methodology may still be at play. The many systematic biases like the subject-allocation bias seen in the birthing-room experiment [3] or the selective recall of the accident-prone aviators could account for results. The increased survival of heart-attack patients who participated in the exercise program [8] and high incidence of abuse and neglect reported among children identified in the nursery as at risk [5] were statistically significant findings, but biases in both studies may make statistical proclamations superfluous. The British statistician, Sir Austin Bradford Hill has remarked that too often, ". . . the glitter of the t-table diverts attention from the inadequacies of the fare" [4].

Summary

Statistical tests need to be kept in proper perspective. Tests of significance only assess the likelihood that sampling variability is responsible for results. They make no other claims on the validity of the study. Clinical significance is still the purview of the physician. Readers who can keep their heads when those about them are lost in a swirl of p-values have an advantage. They can concentrate on issues of relevance.

Ask the following:

1. Are the differences observed between the groups under study likely to be due to chance?

2. If differences are not due to chance, do they occur because of biases or are they related to the treatment or other study factor?

3. If differences are statistically significant (not due to chance), are they clinically important?

4. If differences are not statistically significant, is it possible that a true difference has been overlooked (a type II error made)?

References

1. BERWICK, D. M. Experimental power: The other side of the coin. *Pediatrics* 65:1043–1044, 1980.

2. FREIMAN, J. A., CHALMERS, T. C., SMITH, H., AND KUEBLER, R. R. The importance of beta, the type II error and sample size in the design and interpretation of the randomized control trial. Survey of 71 "negative" trials. *N. Engl. J. Med.* 299:690–694, 1978.

3. GOODLIN, R. C. Low-risk obstetric care for low-risk mothers. *Lancet* 1:1017–1019, 1980.

4. HILL, A. B. The environment and disease: Association or causation? *Proceedings of the Royal Society of Medicine* 58:295–300, 1965.

5. HUNTER, R. S., KILSTROM, N., KRAYBILL, E. N., AND LODA, F. Antecedents of child abuse and neglect in premature infants: A prospective study in a newborn intensive care unit. *Pediatrics* 61:629–635, 1978.

6. KLATSKY, A. L., FRIEDMAN, G. D., SIEGELAUB, A. B., AND GERARD, M. J. Alcohol consumption and blood pressure. *N. Engl. J. Med.* 296:1194–1200, 1977.

7. PLESS, I. B., ROGHMANN, K., AND ALGRANATI, P. The prevention of injuries to children in automobiles. *Pediatrics* 49:420–426, 1972.

8. RECHNITZER, P. A., PICKARD, H. A., PAIVIO, A. U., YUHASZ, M. S., AND CUNNINGHAM, D. Long-term follow-up study of survival and recurrence rates following myocardial infarction in exercising and control subjects. *Circulation* 45:853–856, 1972.

9. REISIN, E., ABEL, R., MODAN, M., SILVERBERG, D. S., ELIAHOU, H. E., AND MODAN, B. Effect of weight loss without salt restriction on the reduction of blood pressure in overweight hypertensive patients. *N. Engl. J. Med.* 298:1–6, 1978.

10. RODDEY, O. F., JR., EARLE, R., JR., AND HAGGERTY, R. Myringotomy in acute otitis media. A controlled study. *JAMA* 197:849–853, 1966.

11. STICKLER, G. B., RUBENSTEIN, M. M., MCBEAN, J. B., HEDGECOCK, L. D., HUGSTAD, J. A., AND GRIFFING, T. Treatment of acute otitis media in children. IV. A fourth clinical trial. *Amer. J. Dis. Child.* 114:123–130, 1967.

NINE

Interpretation: Sensitivity, Specificity, and Predictive Value

F--d has a better idea.
—Well-known advertising slogan

We live with a surfeit of other people's good ideas. The mail brings almost daily suggestions for enriching our medical knowledge while cruising through Caribbean Islands or skiing in the Wasatch Mountains. Journals offer multicolored proposals from pharmaceutical companies for reducing patient blood pressures or relieving contact dermatitis mixed in with the latest epidemiologic pronouncements on the causes of endometrial cancer. Suggestions for improving our diagnostic capabilities also abound. Descriptive studies and cross-sectional designs touting clinical signs and symptoms, laboratory determinations, and radiographic procedures as aids in clinical decision-making are much in vogue. Computerized tomography and ultrasound devices claim to localize lacunae in our heads, holes in our hearts, and cysts in our kidneys. Genetic-typing techniques are available to diagnose ankylosing spondylitis and Down syndrome. Old techniques, such as the Gram stain and the C-reactive protein, are revitalized and used to diagnose streptococcal pharyngitis. Clinical signs and symptoms are combined in different ways in an effort to best predict when stool cultures are likely to yield enteric pathogens. With all the new and not-so-new technological approaches available, it is difficult to decide which dishes among the diagnostic smorgasbord are more worthwhile. In this chapter, we will devote ourselves to interpreting evaluations of these diagnostic ideas.

There are several approaches to assigning value to a new test or symptom complex. The first, which is encountered with distressing frequency, is the author's proclamation that it is so. "In my experience right upper quadrant pain means cholecystitis." "We have found that bilateral infiltrates on chest radiographs signify Legionnaire's disease." The presence of gallbladder disease in eight out of ten patients with abdominal pain, or observation that the last five chest films that had patchy infiltrates had antibody titers to *Legionella* are "swallows that do not a summer make." Many uncontrolled observations filter into the most respected of publications. They may be useful as preliminary, descriptive hunches but should be challenged to provide evidence of validity and generalizability. "Author" and "authority" come from common Middle English stock and run the danger of becoming synonyms in the minds of some. By now a sigh of skepticism should pass our lips on reading that the only proof of value is the investigator's own experience.

A somewhat more satisfactory approach to assessing a new diagnostic technique is to employ a statistical test of association to see if the new method helps discover disease more often than might be expected by chance. The article on blood culturing and bacteremia [5] relies on p-values and statistical significance to support its claims for diagnostic effectiveness. Recall that one of the tidbits of information imparted from this study was that certain clinical and laboratory features were useful predictors of children who were ultimately found to have bacteremia. Among these were age, fever, and white-blood-cell count (see table 9–1).

> Bacteremia was most frequent in children seven to twelve months old ($p < 0.001$) and was associated with a white cell count of 20,000 or more ($p < 0.01$) and a temperature of 39.4°C or higher ($p < 0.01$) [5].

Shunning the seduction of the small p-value and remembering that statistically significant predictors may not be clinically useful guides, we find that table 9–1 provides some helpful information. The frequency of positive blood cultures does rise with temperature as well as with white-blood-cell count and is higher in one of the younger age groups. It also appears that this observation is unlikely to

Table 9–1 Factors Associated with Bacteremia in Outpatient Febrile Children

Factor	Positive Cultures	Total Cultures	Percent Positive
Age (months)			
6 or less	1	74	1.4
7 to 12	11	116	9.5
13 to 24	5	131	3.8
25 or greater	5	225	2.2
Temperature (°C)			
Less than 38.9	2	159	1.3
38.9 to 39.4	4	99	4.0
39.4 to 39.9 (Sic)	10	124	8.1
40.0 or higher	6	96	6.3
White-Blood-Cell Count ($\times 10^3$)			
Less than 10.0	2	162	1.2
10.0 to 19.9	13	193	6.7
20.0 or more	6	52	11.5

Based on data from McGowan, J. E., Jr. et al. [5].

be due to chance. But somehow we are not getting the complete picture. We know something of how valuable the fever and white-blood-cell count are in predicting disease when they are elevated; 12 percent of the time a high white-blood-cell count will identify a patient with bacteremia, 7 percent of the time an elevated temperature will accurately predict the problem. It is also clear, however, that these tests are not always right, only 12 percent and 7 percent of the time. That means that 88 of 100 and 93 of 100 times a high white-blood-cell count and a high fever incorrectly suggest that patients have bacteremia. Furthermore, the tests also fail to detect some patients who have disease. Not every patient who is bacteremic meets the criteria of temperature greater than 39.4°C or white-blood-cell count of more than 20,000. These are important errors in classification and are deficiencies in the tests that clinicians must incorporate into decision-making. Pronouncements of statistical significance alone do not provide sufficient information. Recasting some of the data contained in table 9–1 into the schematic seen in table 9–2

Table 9–2 Factors Associated with Bacteremia in Outpatient Febrile Children

Temperature (Temp)

Temp		Blood Culture		
		Positive	Negative	
	> 39.4°	16	204	220
	< 39.4°	6	252	258
		22	456	478

White-Blood-Cell Count (WBC)

WBC		Blood Culture		
		Positive	Negative	
	≥ 20,000	6	46	52
	< 20,000	15	340	355
		21	386	407

Based on data from McGowan, J. E., Jr. et al. [5].

provides us with a better sense of how the tests are performing. A fever of 39.4°C or greater occurs in 220 of 478 patients. Sixteen of these children turn out to have bacteremia for a frequency of about 7 percent. However, we can see from the table that six children who have positive blood cultures have temperatures below 39.4°C. These children will be misclassified by the criterion of high fever. It is also apparent from inspecting the tables that while 252 of the 456 children who did not have bacteremia are correctly classified by the criterion of fever less than 39.4°C, a substantial number, 204, are incorrectly labelled as bacteremic. Similarly, a white-blood-cell count of greater than 20,000 is an accurate predictor of bacteremia on 6 of 52 occasions, or 12 percent of the time. This test is much more accurate in identifying truly negative patients. In all, 340 of 386 children with negative blood cultures are appropriately classified by virtue of their low white-blood-cell count. Only 46 children with negative blood cultures fall into the high white-blood-cell count group and are incorrectly called bacteremic. This is a much better batting average than the temperature criterion offered. Unfortunately, the white-blood-cell count misses more cases of bacteremia than it identifies. Only 6 of 21 positive cultures have concurrent white-blood-cell counts greater than 20,000; fifteen bacteremia patients have white-blood-cell counts that fall below the cut-off point.

We have just described a systematic approach to evaluating diagnostic tests. Concepts known as sensitivity, specificity, and predictive value, terms familiar to many medical readers, are used to summarize the system. As with other bits of jargon, a moderate amount of confusion has surrounded the application of these terms. Twenty house officers, 20 fourth-year medical students, and 20 attending physicians at four teaching hospitals were asked in "hallway encounters" to solve a medical problem that required calculating the predictive value of a test [2]. Only 11 of the 60 participants were able to come up with the correct answer. The reasoning is straightforward in the sensitivity, specificity, and predictive-value game, but it takes a bit of thought to digest the principles, and for most of us, a pencil and piece of paper for sketching a hasty two-by-two table like the one shown in table 9–3.

Sensitivity is the ability of a test to single out people who have disease. For those who thrive on equations, using the notations in table 9–3, sensitivity is $A/(A + C)$. Specificity is the ability of the test to classify people who do not have illness as negative. In the algebra of

Table 9-3 Sensitivity, Specificity, and Predictive Value

		Disease		
		Present	Absent	
Test	Positive	A	B	A + B
	Negative	C	D	C + D
		A + C	B + D	A + B + C + D

Sensitivity = A/(A + C)

Specificity = D/(B + D)

Predictive Value = A/(A + B)

table 9-3, it is D/(B + D). The predictive value of a diagnostic endeavor gives the frequency with which a positive test actually signifies disease. Reading horizontally across table 9-3, it is A/(A + B). Predictive value is more properly designated as positive predictive value (the value of a positive test). However, as we will see later, its companion, negative predictive value, the frequency with which a negative test identifies people without disease, is substantially less useful. Most authors are speaking positively when they refer to predictive value.

Let us return to the bacteremia data and attach some terms to the information we compiled. Table 9-4 summarizes the sensitivity, specificity, and predictive value for temperature and white-blood-cell count, as diagnostic tests for bacteremia. The two tests may be compared, and the intuitive reservations we developed from examining table 9-2 can be quantified. Using temperature to diagnose bacteremia, we will properly identify 73 percent of patients who have positive cultures. That is the sensitivity. Our specificity is not very high, only 55 percent of patients who are without disease will be properly identified by their position in the lower temperature group. The predictive value of fever is low; only 7 percent of all children with fevers greater than 39.4°C will have positive blood cultures. The specificity of the white-blood-cell count is much better, 88 percent. Sensitivity, however, suffers substantially when this test is used; only 29 percent of children with positive cultures are properly identified. The white-blood-cell count offers better predictive value; of the 52

Table 9–4 Sensitivity, Specificity, and Predictive Value of Temperature and White-Blood-Cell Count in Diagnosing Bacteremia

Temperature (Temp)

	Blood Culture		
	Positive	Negative	
Temp			
< 39.4°	16	204	220
> 39.4°	6	252	258
	22	456	478

Sensitivity = 16/22 = 73%
Specificity = 252/456 = 55%
Predictive Value = 16/220 = 7%

White-Blood-Cell Count (WBC)

	Blood Culture		
	Positive	Negative	
WBC			
≤ 20,000	6	46	52
> 20,000	15	340	355
	21	386	407

Sensitivity = 6/21 = 29%
Specificity = 340/386 = 88%
Predictive Value = 6/52 = 12%

Based on data from McGowan, J. E., Jr. et al. [5].

children with elevated white-blood-cell counts, 12 percent have bacteremia.

There is a message in all this. Diagnostic tests are not perfect. Some degree of misclassification of patients is inevitable. By using attributes of sensitivity, specificity, and predictive value, we are able to quantitate in a standard way the ability of any test to make correct and incorrect classifications. Some papers will speak of the efficiency of a test. Efficiency is an overall estimate of a test's ability to correctly classify patients. The boxes in tables 9–4a and 9–4b surround the numbers of patients who are correctly labelled. Efficiency is the combination of these two correct classification boxes divided by the total number of patients assessed. For temperature this would be (16 + 252)/478 or 56 percent; for white-blood-cell count the efficiency is (6 + 340)/407 or 85 percent.

The concept of efficiency may overly summarize the attributes of the test. White-blood-cell count appears to be a more efficient diagnostic test for detecting bacteremia than temperature. But how concerned is the clinician about missing cases of bacteremia? The high efficiency of white-blood-cell count is due largely to the fact that most patients have negative cultures and also have white-blood-cell counts below 20,000. Over two-thirds of positive cultures are misidentified by using the criteria of the elevated white-blood-cell count. Sensitivity this low is not acceptable. If a disease is worth detecting, a 71 percent miss, or false-negative rate, is unacceptable. Elevated temperature is a more sensitive test; only about one-fourth of patients with positive cultures will fall into the false-negative category. On the other hand, when we choose fever, specificity suffers. Elevated temperatures were seen in 204 of the 456 patients with negative cultures. These are false positives, people the test falsely accuses of having disease.

A Practical Example

Before heads swirl from terminology overload, let us try another example. Suppose we have just taken on the job of emergency-room clinician in a hospital in the rolling piedmont of North Carolina. In the process of orienting ourselves to diseases indigenous to the area, we learn that the region leads all others in the incidence of Rocky Mountain spotted fever (RMSF). Blowing the cobwebs from our infectious-disease text, we recall that RMSF is a rickettsial disease transmitted by ticks. Patients suffering from the illness complain of severe frontal headache, high fever, and myalgias. Three or four days into the illness they break out with a macular rash that involves the palms and soles and is the hallmark of the disease. Since the illness can be fatal if left untreated, it is an important diagnosis to make. However, we learn from some emergency-room colleagues that diagnosis is not always easy. Patients who come in with fever, aches, and pains before the rash begins may have any of a number of summer viruses. Serologic tests are available to make the diagnosis, but it is five to ten days into the illness before the antibody response can be detected. In short, we have a diagnostic dilemma: how do you spot RMSF in time to offer prompt, effective therapy?

It turns out, a group of astute colleagues who have been studying the disease at a nearby medical center have collected some interesting information. They have observed that serum sodium is abnormally low in 50 percent of patients who are ultimately diagnosed as having RMSF. This is a "highly significant" association. Since serum-sodium determinations are readily available and can be obtained and interpreted in the emergency room, the test is being suggested as a diagnostic aid in the identification of RMSF. Sounds promising, but does the test measure up?

Of our new tools, sensitivity, specificity, and predictive value, one is already at hand. Of patients who have RMSF, 50 percent will have a sodium serum of 130 meq or less. That is the sensitivity of the test. It also means, of course, that 50 percent of patients who have the disease will be missed if the electrolyte determination is relied upon as the only arbiter of disease (false negatives). We are lacking information that enables us to calculate specificity or predictive value. We need to know the frequency with which a low serum-sodium determination occurs in people who do not have RMSF. Since that information does not appear in the reference materials we have at hand, we decide to conduct a survey in our own emergency room. Electrolyte determinations are made on the next 100 patients who visit, and we find that 2 percent of them have serum-sodium values below 130 meq. These are false-positive values for the test and as seen in table 9–5 mean that the specificity is 98 percent. It looks as if the test is proving its merit. Fifty of 100 cases of RMSF are correctly identified and 98 of 100 without the disease are also properly designated. What of the predictive value?

Table 9–5   Serum Sodium and Rocky Mountain Spotted Fever

		Rocky Mountain Spotted Fever		
		Present	*Absent*	
Serum Sodium	≤ 130	50	2	
	> 130	50	98	
		100	100	200

Sensitivity	=	50/100 = 50%
Specificity	=	98/100 = 98%
Predictive Value	=	?

It would appear from reading the top row of table 9–5, that 50 of 52 times (96 percent) a low serum sodium is indicative of RMSF. That is a potent predictive value, but it does not seem quite right. Something is missing! Inspection of the bottom row of table 9–5, which shows the total cases evaluated, reveals the problem. Reading across, the row suggests that 100 of 200 patients evaluated had RMSF. That is a rather startling frequency for any disease. We need a better estimate of the prevalence of the disease in our emergency-room population. The predictive value of any test depends upon the prevalence of the disease. When sensitivity and specificity of diagnostic tests are calculated by independently examining a group of cases and a group of controls without accounting for the overall disease frequency, predictive value cannot be calculated. Either prevalence must be estimated from other information, or we must derive it from the population we have at hand.

To estimate the frequency with which RMSF occurs in our setting, we review the charts of all patients seen in our emergency room during the past year. We find 5 RMSF cases diagnosed among 5,000 patient visits for a rate of 1 case per 1,000 patients per year. That alters our estimate of predictive value substantially, as table 9–6 shows. Now for every 100 cases of RMSF there will be 99,900 people without the disease; and with the same specificity of 98 percent (a false-positive rate of only 2 percent), the predictive value plummets to just about 2 percent. This is a cold splash of water indeed, but a point that is worth remembering. Most diseases occur

Table 9–6 Serum Sodium and Rocky Mountain Spotted Fever Among All Emergency-Room Patients

		Rocky Mountain Spotted Fever		
		Present	*Absent*	
Serum Sodium	≤ 130	50	1,998	2,048
	> 130	50	97,902	
		100	99,900	100,000

Sensitivity	=	50/100 = 50%
Specificity	=	97,902/99,900 = 98%
Predictive Value	=	50/2,048 = 2.4%
Prevalence	=	1/1,000

infrequently. When the prevalence is low, even tests with relatively high specificity will produce a substantial number of false positives. This imbalance, as demonstrated in table 9–6, results in a much lower predictive value than most clinicians would anticipate. Only 2 or 3 people of every 100 that come to our emergency room and have a low serum sodium will have RMSF.

Ruling In and Ruling Out Disease

When clinicians order a test or evaluate clinical sign, they like to interpret it as being either positive or negative. The serum sodium is above or below 130 meq, antinuclear antibody is present or absent, the tip of the spleen is felt or is not detected. We use these dichotomized results in two ways. In the ungainly vernacular of the profession, we are constantly trying to rule in or rule out disease. If a test, symptom, or sign is positive, what is the likelihood that the patient has disease? Can disease be ruled in? If the test or observation is negative, how sure can we be that the patient does not have disease? Can it be ruled out? Predictive value provides us with the information we need to rule in an illness. It is pretty straightforward.

Ruling out disease is a little trickier. One's initial temptation would be to look at the negative predictive value, the likelihood that a negative result means the patient is free of disease. From the data shown in table 9–6 a serum sodium of greater than 130 meq would appear to give us great confidence in ruling out RMSF; the negative predictive value is 97902/97952 or 99.9 percent. Such comfort is misleading, however. Remember that RMSF is an uncommon disease. It occurs in only 1 of every 1,000 patients that come to the emergency room. That means we already know that most people with serum sodium above 130 meq do not have RMSF. The 99.9 percent figure promotes false security. The information needed to determine rule-out properties of a test is best provided by sensitivity. Our serum-sodium guidelines correctly identify cases of RMSF only 50 percent of the time. Few of us would harbor delusions of diagnostic grandeur and claim to have ruled out RMSF knowing that we would be missing 50 percent of the cases.

Suppose our data looked like the data presented in table 9–7. The specificity of our test has remained the same (98 percent), but we have been able to raise the sensitivity to 98 percent as well. The negative predictive value has changed very little. It is still about 99.9 percent, but with a sensitivity as high as 98 percent, the test has become much more useful as a means to rule out disease. Now only

Table 9–7 Serum Sodium and Rocky Mountain Spotted Fever Among All Emergency-Room Patients

		Rocky Mountain Spotted Fever		
		Present	*Absent*	
Serum Sodium	≤ 130	98	1,998	2,096
	> 130	2	97,902	
		100	99,900	100,000

Sensitivity	= 98/100 = 98%
Specificity	= 97,902/99,900 = 98%
Predictive Value	= 98/2,096 = 4.7%
Prevalence	= 1/1,000

2 of every 100 cases will be missed, and we can say with reasonable confidence that a negative test substantially rules out RMSF.

Improving Predictive Value

We are still left with the problem that predictive values are low when illnesses are uncommon. With sensitivity and specificity both at 98 percent, the predictive value in table 9–7 is still only 4.7 percent. To improve predictive value, we need to increase the prevalence of disease. While this seems to imply an assault on the higher order of things, clinicians increase prevalence every day. They do it by combining symptoms, signs, and laboratory tests to discover subsets of patients who have a greater likelihood of having disease. It is the essence of clinical diagnosis. Let us think back on how we determined the prevalence of RMSF in our emergency-room population. We took the 5 cases of RMSF from the total 5,000 visits to the emergency room. We could easily have been more selective. Within those 5,000 patient visits were many encounters for problems not remotely resembling RMSF. Bumped heads, lacerated fingers, and patients with substernal chest pain were included in the total. The most compulsive of clinicians would not entertain the thought of RMSF in the differential diagnoses of most of these patients, let alone order a serum sodium for purposes of ruling in the disease. A much more lucrative subsample to evaluate would be patients who were suspected of having an infectious disease, who, for example, had fever. Suppose we restrict ourselves to assessing febrile patients. Our data might now look much like the data in table 9–8. It turns out that only 500 of the total 5,000 visits were made by patients with fever. Since it is unlikely that anyone would make the diagnosis of RMSF in the absence of fever, we can recalculate the disease prevalence as 5 in 500 or 1 percent. It looks as if predictive value is going to improve. However, we do need to recall that our estimate of specificity came from assessing a general group of emergency-room patients and was not limited to those with fever. Because other, nonrickettsial infectious diseases could produce some electrolyte abnormalities, we may find the specificity of our test falls slightly when applied only to patients with fever. Suppose that 5 percent of patients who have fever, but not RMSF, have sodium values below 130 meq.

Table 9-8 Serum Sodium and Rocky Mountain Spotted Fever Among Patients with Fever

		Rocky Mountain Spotted Fever		
		Present	*Absent*	
Serum Sodium	≤ 130	50	495	545
	> 130	50	9,405	
		100	9,900	10,000

Sensitivity	=	50/100 = 50%
Specificity	=	9,405/9,900 = 95%
Predictive Value	=	50/545 = 9.2%
Prevalence	=	1/100

Even though the specificity has fallen to 95 percent, the effect of increasing the prevalence has greatly augmented our predictive value. It has risen from 2.4 percent to 9.2 percent (compare table 9-6 with table 9-8). We could further improve our predictive value by using subpopulations of the original emergency-room group to test. Testing could be restricted not only to people with fever but to those who also complain of headache and give a history of a recent tick bite. This would greatly reduce the number of people we consider for electrolyte testing and increase the prevalence of disease; but as we add selective criteria, we take some additional diagnostic risks. The assumption that fever is universally present in patients with RMSF is reasonable; but headache is present only 80 percent of the time, and only 50 percent of people who are subsequently diagnosed as having the disease report tick exposure. Sensitivity begins to erode with addition of these criteria. If the probability that RMSF patients have fever is 1.0, have a headache is 0.8, and a tick bite, 0.5, the likelihood of all three independent events occurring is 0.4 (1.0 × 0.8 × 0.5). In other words, only 40 of 100 patients with the disease will remain eligible for serum-sodium determination when all criteria are used as a screen. If sensitivity remains 50 percent in this subgroup, only one-half of these 40 patients will be identified as having RMSF, or 20 percent of the original 100 cases. Even if prevalence rises to a

Table 9–9 Serum Sodium and Rocky Mountain Spotted Fever Among Patients with Fever, Headache, and History of Tick Bite

		Rocky Mountain Spotted Fever	
		Present	*Absent*
Serum Sodium	≤ 130	20	10
	> 130	20	90
		40 (+60 excluded) = 100	100 │ 200
	Sensitivity	= 20/40 = 50%	
	Specificity	= 90/100 = 90%	
	Predictive Value	= 20/30 = 67%	
	Prevalence	= 1/2	

hefty 50 percent under these conditions and specificity remains high at 90 percent, our capacity to rule in disease (predictive value) is just 67 percent (20/30) not the 83 percent (50/60) we might have anticipated. Table 9–9 depicts this.

Making Choices

The game of diagnostics is one of tradeoffs. When we attempt to improve the sensitivity of our procedures and detect everyone who has an illness, we become less selective. We fall back to the most common denominator, like fever, and include people who do not have the disease. We can become more restrictive, by raising the specificity of the test and reducing the number of false-positive determinations. But sensitivity is bound to suffer.

This tradeoff process is illustrated in figure 9–1. The figure depicts two overlapping distributions. One represents the values for serum sodium in patients with confirmed RMSF; the other distribution shows serum-sodium values for febrile patients without the disease. By changing the cut point that divides a positive and negative test, sensitivity and specificity can be altered. If the value of 130 meq

Rocky Mountain Spotted Fever (RMSF)

		Present	Absent	
	122			
	123	X		
	124	X		
	125	XX		
	126	XX		
	127			
	128	XXX	XX	
	129	X	X	
	130	------------------------------		D₁
Serum	131	XX		
	132		x	
Sodium	133	XX	X	
	134	XXX	XX	
(Na)	135	. . . . .X.	.XX.	D₂
	136		XXX	
	137	X		
	138	X	XXXX	
	139			
	140		XXX	
	141			
	142		X	

Decision Point—D₁			
		RMSF	
		Present	Absent
Na	≤130	10	3
	>130	10	17
		20	20

Sensitivity = 10/20 = 50%
Specificity = 17/20 = 85%

Decision Point—D₂			
		RMSF	
		Present	Absent
Na	≤135	18	9
	>135	2	11
		20	20

Sensitivity = 18/20 = 90%
Specificity = 11/20 = 55%

Figure 9–1. *Distribution of serum-sodium (Na) values for subjects with and without Rocky Mountain spotted fever. Sensitivity and specificity differ depending on which of two decision points (D_1 or D_2) is used.*

or less is used to designate a positive test, the sensitivity in detecting RMSF will be 50 percent (10/20); specificity under these conditions will be 85 percent (17/20). To improve sensitivity, we can move the cut point to a higher serum-sodium value. If 135 meq or less is used to diagnose RMSF, sensitivity rises to 90 percent (18/20), but specificity will suffer, falling to 55 percent (11/20). We just cannot have our cake both ways.

Nevertheless, choices between sensitivity and specificity must be made. How do we decide where to cut the line between positive and negative and between sensitivity and specificity? The answer is not a statistical one. It is a clinical and economic decision. What are the costs of misclassifying patients? When the consequences of missing a disease are crucial as in the case of a curable cancer or treatable, life-threatening bacterial infection, sensitivity is paramount. We are willing to risk misclassifying a few people as positives, especially if other more definitive diagnostic procedures are available to correct our initial mistakes.

Screening programs to detect phenylketonuria (PKU) among newborns attempt to be very sensitive. Failure to detect cases of this treatable genetic disease will result in permanent mental retardation and great personal and social cost. A percentage of false positives will occur in these screening programs, but repeat blood tests are readily available to correctly reclassify these babies.

If, on the other hand, the burden of creating false positives outweighs the advantages of capturing all cases of a disease, increasing specificity should be the goal. If exploratory surgery or invasive angiography is necessary to confirm a diagnosis, high specificity is desirable. An example of a clinical sign that is frequently encountered and should be specific is the heart murmur. While heart murmurs can be a reasonably sensitive diagnostic aid for detecting valvular heart disease (most people with bad valves have murmurs), there are many people who have heart murmurs and perfectly normal hearts (false positives). Substantial medical costs can be incurred if extensive cardiac evaluation is performed on every patient who has a murmur. Thousands of cardiograms, chest x-rays, and even catheterizations can be done to document the absence of heart disease in patients misclassified by the presence of a murmur. Bergman and Stamm have even written about the psychological effects that can occur when children with "innocent" heart murmurs are thought by parents to be suffering from heart disease [1]. Activities become restricted as children are put into undesirable sick roles by diagnostic misclassification.

One remedy for this kind of problem is to increase the specificity of one's cardiac evaluation. Classifying the murmur by location, duration, occurrence in the cardiac cycle, and so on can improve specificity and lower the number of false positives.

Let us recap the basics covered thus far. We have seen that for assessing the diagnostic worth of tests, proclamations of highly statistically significant associations are not sufficient. P-values may cover the page and not tell us what we want to know. Clinicians need information on the extent to which diagnostic tests misclassify subjects. Characteristics like sensitivity, specificity, and predictive value are tools necessary to making clinical decisions. We can learn the probability that tests will miss cases of disease (false negatives) and how likely it is a positive result will occur in a patient who is free of disease (false positives). In predictive value we have an estimate of the likelihood that given a positive test, a patient will in fact have the illness in question. We have seen that predictive value is at the mercy of prevalence: even a small percentage of false positives becomes magnified when a disease is rare and reduces the likelihood that a positive test signifies disease. We have seen that the sensitivity and specificity of tests can change as decision points are altered. In some cases a test must be highly sensitive in order to identify all cases of illness and specificity is sacrificed. In other instances the costs of creating false positives are intolerable and specificity must be preserved at the expense of sensitivity.

Spectrum

Variations in the prevalence of a disease influence the utility of a test, but sensitivity and specificity may also vary, depending on the clinical stage of disease. A test that appears useful in an advanced state of illness may be less useful early in the disease course. Ransohoff and Feinstein refer to this as the problem of spectrum [6]. Diseases are dynamic and heterogeneous in nature and present a range of manifestations and bodily reactions as they progress. The interactions between host and disease are different in early stages of colon cancer, rheumatoid arthritis, or bacterial endocarditis from those that occur later in the course of illness. Tests that reflect the physiology or immune response of patients with overt, symptomatic illness may have little value in preclinical cases.

A case in point is the serum sodium. All the while we have been fussing about ways to make this diagnostic test useful in identifying cases of RMSF, we have been holding to an assumption that is likely to be untrue. Our problem from the outset was to diagnose cases of RMSF in their early stages, when patients had fever and headache but prior to the development of the rash and more severe complications. However, the information we received about the association between electrolyte abnormalities and the illness was obtained from hospitalized patients. These patients were, in all likelihood, moderately to severely ill and had been ill long enough to make the diagnosis clear. Can we assume their electrolytes are behaving like those of patients who are only a day or two into the illness? Probably not. If low serum sodium is a reflection of the progressive vasculitis of RMSF, it seems unlikely that the electrolyte problems noted late in the disease are present with the same frequency early on. This disease has a spectrum, and the test we are evaluating may vary in value depending on where in the course of illness we apply it.

Documentation of the problem of spectrum and diagnostic-test utility comes from the literature on screening tests for prostatic cancer. Authors of one study evaluated a radioimmunoassay for prostatic acid phosphatase in hopes it would detect the disease early in its course when treatment would be more effective [3]. Unfortunately, they found that the value of the test varied with the stage of progression of the cancer. In later stages of the disease the test had reasonably high sensitivity. It identified between 71 percent and 92 percent of cancer patients. However, in the earlier Stage I of the disease, only one-third of patients with known prostate cancer tested positive. The problem of spectrum is an important one. It has a surprisingly similar flavor to the whole business of population selection that has recurred so frequently throughout the book.

Standards

To this point we have devoted much discussion to the diagnostic tests or clinical signs being evaluated, but paid little mind to the standards against which tests are compared. We have taken for granted that we really knew who had RMSF, prostate cancer, or bacteremia. How do we know who truly has disease and who does not? Are the standards against which we measure tests true? The answer of course depends on which standard we use, since standards vary widely. Sometimes biopsy and histologic examination are utilized, other times serology, still other tests are validated by combinations of clinical impressions and laboratory or radiologic determinations. It should be remembered that all these methods have their own limitations and rates of error. Pathologists can misinterpret histologic sections, serologic tests may in themselves lack sufficient sensitivity to uniformly detect disease, and clinical impressions are woefully susceptible to observer error.

Familiar principles from previous chapters should rattle in our ears. Standards are diagnostic endpoints and, like entry criteria, treatment descriptions, and other determinations of outcome, must be clearly and satisfactorily defined. Biases can be introduced by observers who know of the test results before they read histologic sections or count colonies on the confirming culture. Conversely, knowledge of the true diagnosis may influence the interpretation of radiologic scans or physical-examination findings. Watch for these. Test results may affect the rigor with which standards are applied. When a test is positive, clinicians will look harder to find disease than when results are negative. More tests are ordered, additional x-rays obtained, exploratory surgery is undertaken. Standard are unevenly applied. Often this cannot be avoided since it is difficult to subject patients to invasive and expensive procedures without some justification.

Evaluations of breast-cancer-screening programs are hampered by the uneven assessment of truth brought about by this work-up bias. When techniques like mammography are assessed as screening tests for breast cancer, the standard is determined by biopsy. Women with suspicious lesions will have histologic diagnoses made. True positives and false positives can be reasonably estimated. We will have a good idea of the test's predictive value. Valid estimates of sensitivity will be much less satisfactory. Women for whom mammograpy is negative are not biopsied to find malignancies unless some other tests hint at the presence of a lesion. Yet, some undetected cancers are certain to exist. These will be false negatives that will go unappreciated because we are unable to apply our standard uniformly. Even when alternative tests turn up cancers that mammography fails to find, our best guess of sensitivity will remain an overestimate.

For many diseases, a single, valid standard is not available. Take heart attack for example. Without autopsy evidence of coronary occlusion and tissue death, the diagnosis of myocardial infarction must be made on a combination of clinical and laboratory features. Most clinicians rely on history of chest pain, evidence of disturbed myocardial rhythm or function, the results of the electrocardiogram, and a variety of serum-enzyme determinations to make the decision whether or not a patient has had a heart attack. While using a combination of clinical and laboratory observations is a perfectly legitimate diagnostic technique, it is not permissible to use the results of the test being evaluated as part of the standard. Surprisingly enough, this has been done. Studies have described the utility of particular muscle enzyme patterns in predicting myocardial infarction and included in the criteria for truth, clinical impressions that incorporate the enzyme results. It is not surprising to find reasonably good sensitivity for a test that is both predictor and standard.

Practical Considerations

Let us work through one last example to explore the practical use of sensitivity, specificity, and predictive value in clinical decision-making. Streptococcal sore throat presents a nagging problem for clinicians. It seems the more we learn about streptococcal pharyngitis, the more complicated things become. It is now appreciated that not every patient who complains of sore throat and has streptococci isolated from a throat swab is at risk of developing post-streptococcal sequelae, such as rheumatic fever. Some people appear to be chronic carriers of streptococcus. Evidence for this comes from the fact that a substantial number of individuals who harbor the organism in their throats do not show streptococcal antibody titer changes. In these individuals, the streptococcus does not appear to be causing infection but is simply along for the ride.

If carriers of the germ are really not susceptible to the complications of streptococcal sore throat, it may be worthwhile to identify these people and spare them unnecessary fretting and unnecessary administration of antibiotics. Investigators from Minneapolis tested the observation that an "acute phase reactant," the C-reactive protein (CRP) might be a good predictor of actual infection by the streptococcus [4]. The CRP is a serum protein that can be assessed from a blood specimen taken at the time a patient is seen for the sore throat.

For the study, these investigators chose 157 patients who had symptoms of sore throat and throat cultures positive for Group A beta streptococci. Each patient had a CRP determination made and an acute and convalescent titer to two antistreptococcal antibodies [the antistreptolycin-O (ASO) and the antistreptococcal deoxyribonuclease B (anti-DNase B)] drawn. The ASO and the anti-DNase B represent the standard. Elevations in the CRP were compared against increased titers in these antistreptococcal antibodies.

The summary of results offers a good opportunity for practicing diagnostic-test assessment. They report:

> In the group of 157 patients reported here, 69 (44 percent) demonstrated a significant rise in ASO and/or anti-DNase B titer. Of these 69 patients, 54 (78%) had a positive CRP test at the initial visit . . . 101 of the 157 patients (64 percent) had a positive CRP test at the initial visit. Of those with the positive CRP test, 53 percent subsequently demonstrated a significant rise in ASO and/or anti-DNase B. In contrast, only about one quarter (15/56) of those with a negative CRP test had a significant rise in streptococcal antibody titers.

The authors conclude that:

> The CRP test falls short of being a perfect predictor of which patients with pharyngitis and a positive culture will develop an antibody response. However, the data do strongly suggest this laboratory test may be helpful to the clinician, especially if the CRP determination is negative at the initial visit.

How does one go about getting a reasonable idea of whether or not the conclusion is reasonable and CRP is a useful adjunct to the diagnosis and treatment of streptococcal pharyngitis? The first step is to construct a table that orders the data in a way that we can easily visualize and calculate the sensitivity, specificity, and predictive value. This is done in table 9–10. With a sensitivity of 78 percent and a specificity of 47 percent, the test is modestly successful in effectively differentiating streptococcal carriers from those infected with the organism. But is the CRP worthwhle? To answer this question we need to balance benefits that may result from implementing the new test against the standard practices for dealing with streptococcal sore throat.

The usual procedure for dealing with patients who complain of sore throat and have a positive throat culture is to ply them with ten days of penicillin. This is a relatively inexpensive, low-risk treatment with documented efficacy in preventing rheumatic fever. The draw-

Table 9–10   C-Reactive Protein (CRP) in Culture-Proven Streptococcal Pharyngitis

		Antibody Rise		
		Positive (infected)	Negative (carrier)	
CRP	Positive	54	47	101
	Negative	15	41	56
		69	88	157
	Sensitivity	= 54/69 = 78%		
	Specificity	= 41/88 = 47%		
	Predictive Value	= 54/101 = 53%		

Based on Kaplan, E. L. and Wannamaker, L. W. [4] by permission of the American Academy of Pediatrics.

back, as the data we have acquired in this study show, is that over one-half the people who have positive throat cultures are carriers rather than infected individuals. This means that we are subjecting a substantial number of people to the allergy risks of penicillin unnecessarily. If we elect to treat everyone as Option 1 in table 9–11 suggests, 56 percent (88/157) of patients would get unwarranted treatment. At the same time, all 69 patients who require penicillin get it.

Utilizing the CRP test would reduce this overtreatment. From Option 2 in table 9–11, we see that of the 88 patients who are carriers, 41 would have negative CRP tests and could be spared the penicillin. Because the test is not perfect, however, 47 patients fall into the false positive category and would be incorrectly identified as infected and treated anyway. On the other hand, the disadvantage of the CRP is that 15 patients who have streptococcal infections requiring treatment would be missed. Thus, while 47 percent of patients who do not need it benefit by not getting penicillin, 22 percent of the 69 people who need therapy do not receive it. For the clinician, the trade becomes the risks of rheumatic fever and spread of streptococcus against the possibility of penicillin allergy. It is an interesting decision.

Table 9–11   Options for Treating Culture-Proven Streptococcal
Pharyngitis

Option 1   Treat all positive cultures—Total 157

	Antibody Rise	
	positive (infected)	negative (carrier)
	Rx-necessary (69)	Rx-unnecessary (88)

Cost: Penicillin, 157 courses at $5/course = $785

Risk: Unnecessary penicillin exposure, 88 people

Benefit: All infected cases treated

Option 2   Treat only C-reactive protein (CRP) positive cases—Total 101

		Antibody Rise	
		positive (infected)	negative (carrier)
CRP	positive	Rx-necessary (54)	Rx-unnecessary (47)
	negative	No Rx-necessary (15)	No Rx-unnecessary (41)
		69	88

Cost: Penicillin, 101 courses at $5/course   = $ 505
         CRP test, 157 tests at $5 each   =   785
                                        TOTAL = $1290

Risk: Fail to treat infected cases, 15 people

Benefit: Reduce unnecessary penicillin exposure, 41 people

The cost of doing additional testing also figures into the evaluation. If we assume that both the CRP test and a ten-day course of penicillin cost approximately $5.00, what would be the economic implications of routinely using CRP testing? Going by the standard approach and giving all 157 patients penicillin at $5 a crack the total cost is $785. If we use the CRP diagnostic adjunct we save on penicillin costs. Only 101 of the 157 patients will get penicillin prescriptions, which is a bill of only $505. Unfortunately, the savings in penicillin are swallowed up by the $785 necessary to perform the 157 CRP determinations. Averaging the patient costs the price per patient for the CRP program is a little over $8 compared to $5 for the standard give-them-all-penicillin approach. Overall, it is difficult to justify CRP testing. It increases the cost of treating streptococcal pharyngitis by 64 percent and leaves the clinician with the dilemma of choosing between saving 26% of patients from unnecessary penicillin exposure and failing to treat 22% of people who have infected sore throats. Practical, on-line application is the bottom line in evaluating the utility of a diagnostic test. Does application result in improved medical care? Is the disease detected more frequently, at lower cost, and with fewer false positives than by existing methods?

Sensitivity, specificity, and predictive value are tools for clinicians to evaluate the cornucopia of diagnostic offerings described in medical journals. In the final analysis, the clinician must decide whether taking on a new test is beneficial. Clinical benefits must be weighed against medical risks and financial liabilities. Do blood cultures really improve the ability to identify seriously ill children? Do costs of performing CAT scans on patients with headaches pay off? Does the poor specificity of mammography, which results in biopsy of many women without malignant breast disease, negate its value as a diagnostic test? These are difficult questions, but it is essential that every new diagnostic test undergo rigorous scrutiny. If the test does not do it better or less expensively, it is not worth using.

Summary

When articles offer information on new diagnostic tests, new applications of old tests, or novel ways of utilizing clinical symptoms and signs to identify diseases, ask the following:

1. Have sensitivity, specificity, and predictive value been calculated? Do the authors give evidence that they understand the importance of misclassifying patients into disease (false positive) or nondisease (false negative) categories? Has predictive value been correctly ascertained with reference to the prevalence of the disease in the population?

2. Has the problem of spectrum been considered? Do subjects on whom a test's sensitivity and specificity are being determined have severe or late-stage manifestations of disease? Are the results of tests on these individuals likely to apply to subjects who are less ill?

3. Is a reasonable standard being used? Are the histological, serological, or clinical impressions used to measure the test's validity reasonable proxies of truth? Have standards been applied equally to all patients in the evaluation? If not everyone has had an x-ray or blood test, have patients who truly have disease been missed? Have authors avoided the temptation to include the test being evaluated as part of the standard? Have they guarded against bias by keeping standard evaluators protected from the influence of knowing test results?

4. Does the test improve on the present state of affairs? Is it more accurate, less costly, less painful, less time consuming, or in some other way better than the diagnostic techniques currently in practice?

References

1. BERGMAN, A. B. AND STAMM, S. J. The morbidity of cardiac non-disease in schoolchildren. *N. Engl. J. Med.* 276:1008–1013, 1967.

2. CASSCELLS, W., SCHOENBERGER, A., AND GRABOYS, T. B. Interpretation by physicians of clinical laboratory results. *N. Engl. J. Med.* 299:999–1001, 1978.

3. FOTI, A. G., COOPER, J. F., HERSCHMYAN, H., AND MALVAEX, R. R. Detection of prostatic cancer by solid-phase radioimmunoassay of serum prostatic acid phosphatase. *N. Engl. J. Med.* 297:1357–1361, 1977.

4. KAPLAN, E. L. AND WANNAMAKER, L. W. C-reactive protein in streptococcal pharyngitis. *Pediatrics* 60:28–32, 1977.

5. MCGOWAN, J. E., JR., BRATTON, L., KLEIN, J. O., AND FINLAND, M. Bacteremia in febrile children seen in a "walk-in" pediatric clinic. *N. Engl. J. Med.* 288:1309–1312, 1973.

6. RANSOHOFF, D. F. AND FEINSTEIN, A. R. Problems of spectrum and bias in evaluating the efficacy of diagnostic tests. *N. Engl. J. Med.* 299:926–930, 1978.

TEN

Interpretation: Risk

Beware the Jabberwock, my son!
The jaws that bite, the claws that catch!
Beware the Jubjub bird, and shun
The frumious Bandersnatch!
—*Lewis Carroll*, Through the Looking Glass

Risks lurk everywhere. Inhaling pollutants puts patients with bronchitis at risk of exacerbation. Placing a foot down on the accelerator pedal of our Porsche increases the risk of automotive mortality. Consuming nitrite preservatives and food dyes may predispose us to cancer. Gulping down chloramphenicol to ward off the Rocky Mountain spotted fever contracted in chapter 9 invites risk of aplastic anemia. Simply belonging to a family where heart disease or diabetes prevails can increase our chances of developing these diseases later in life.

Clinicians are faced with scores of implicit risks each day. They must constantly balance the benefits of treatment plans against potential liabilities. How likely is a 21-year-old primigravida with elevated blood pressure and proteinuria to develop eclampsia at delivery? What's the probability a child with a febrile convulsion will develop epilepsy? What do you tell a 49-year-old with gallbladder disease about chances of surviving a cholecystectomy? Although the numbers are not always there to quantitate the choices, the use of risk to weigh therapeutic choices and estimate future events occurs constantly in the clinical setting.

Risk serves several additional purposes in journal articles. Researchers use comparative risks to unravel the etiology of diseases, such as toxic-shock syndrome and breast cancer, or to demonstrate the effectiveness of interventions such as vaccination or INH prophy-laxis in preventing polio and tuberculosis. Public-health planners gauge the risks of venereal diseases or drug abuse among subgroups of our population in order to focus their intervention efforts.

In this chapter we will examine the concept of risk as it is presented in medical journals and try to make a potential Jabber-wock less intimidating.

Statements of Risk

Basic risk statements express the likelihood that a par-ticular event will occur within a particular population, for example, the number of cases of aplastic anemia among patients taking chloramphenicol or the frequency with which Down syndrome will occur in babies born to women over 40 years old. The virtue of the basic risk statement lies with its denominator: the number of people at risk. All too often when we read of medical events we learn only of the numerators, that is, of the patients who developed aplastic anemia or who came down with toxic-shock syndrome. Knowing the denominators helps. Despite the adverse publicity directed at chloramphenicol, aplastic anemia occurs only once in every 30,000 to 40,000 doses [8]. Notwithstanding the flurry of controversy sur-rounding toxic-shock syndrome and tampon use, the risk of de-veloping the disease is on the order of only 6 cases for every 100,000 menstruating women per year [5]. Risks are proportions that keep medical adversities in their place.

Not surprisingly, our best estimates of risk come from follow-up studies that observe cohorts of people and monitor their outcomes. Natural-history studies that watch for the frequency of renal com-plications in schoolgirls with bacteriuria or the development of postpartum depression among women who have lost infants offer estimates of risk that provide valuable guides for prognosis and management.

Relative Risk

Much that is published in medical journals concerns not simply the natural history of things but the quest for explanations. What are the causes of disease, and what steps can modern medicine take to reduce the likelihood of disability and death? In the search for etiology there are specific ways of defining and comparing risks. Readers will encounter terms, such as relative risk, relative odds, risk ratio, and odds ratio, as descriptors that attempt to get at the causes of disease. The relative risk compares the likelihood that a disease or outcome will occur among individuals who have a particular characteristic, exposure, or risk factor with the likelihood that the outcome will occur in individuals who do not have it. The higher the ratio, the stronger the association between the factor and the disease. Let us consider some examples.

The search for causes of coronary artery disease has been a medical obsession for some years. A host of factors ranging from eating, drinking, and smoking habits to blood pressure and cholesterol levels to genetic attributes have been examined in an attempt to increase our understanding of the disease. Among the more interesting studies are those demonstrating increased risk of heart disease among men who exhibit certain personality characteristics. A so-called coronary-prone behavior pattern or type-A personality has been characterized by:

> competitiveness, striving for achievement, aggressiveness, time urgency, restlessness, hyperalertness, explosiveness of speech amplitude, tenseness of facial musculature and feelings of struggle against the limitations of time and insensitivity of the environment. This torrent of life is usually, but not always, channeled into a vocation or profession with such dedication that type-A persons often neglect other aspects of their life such as family and recreation [10].

In a follow-up study of 2,700 men conducted in the mid-1960s [10], subjects completed questionnaires to provide information on the presence of these type-A characteristics. Subjects were ranked by behavior scores and followed for four years to see who developed coronary artery disease. The annual risk of heart disease among men who exhibited the highest number of type-A behavioral attributes was 14.3 per 1,000 compared to 8.0 per 1,000 for men with calmer behavior. Men with intermediate scores showed an intermediate rate. Comparing the risks for the highest and lowest scores, a relative risk of 14.3/1,000 ÷ 8/1,000 or 1.8 is obtained. In other words, men exhibiting a high degree of type-A behavior were almost twice as likely to develop heart disease during the follow-up period as men without these characteristics. Personality appears to have a role in causes of heart disease.

Risk need not be viewed in negative terms. Other investigators who were looking for factors that would predict survival of patients who were discharged from a coronary-care unit discovered that the support offered by "animal companions" provided protection from mortality [7]. Ninety-two men and women who were recovering from heart attacks or bouts of angina pectoris supplied information on a broad range of personal topics, including pet ownership. A year after hospitalization follow-up was made to discover the status of the patients. Fourteen of the 92 had died. When death rates were calculated according to pet ownership, only 3 of 53 pet owners (5.6 percent) were no longer living compared with 11 of 39 (28 percent) patients who were without animal companions. The relative risk of 5.6 per 100 ÷ 28 per 100, or 0.2 means only one-fifth the mortality or a 5-fold greater likelihood of survival, if one has a furry or a feathered friend. That's an impressive difference! Perhaps prescriptions for Dachshunds rather than digitalis should be offered at discharge from coronary-care units.

Relative Risk and Study Design

When we start with a population, as we do in follow-up studies, the calculation of relative risk is straightforward. We know in advance who eats carrots and who does not. We classify these people and remeasure them later to see who has developed poor eyesight. Table 10–1 illustrates how relative risk is created when the prevalence of disease in the population is known.

Case-control studies are trickier. Since the design enlists patients who already have poor vision, sorts them according to who consumes carrots, and makes the comparison with an independently selected control group, a common population base is lacking. The true risk of disease cannot be calculated. We need to know about the

Table 10–1 Relative Risk in Population-Based (Follow-Up) Studies

	Disease Present	Disease Absent	
Factor Present	A	B	A + B
Factor Absent	C	D	C + D

$$\text{Relative Risk} = \frac{\text{rate of disease in people with factor}}{\text{rate of disease in people without factor}}$$

$$= \frac{\text{disease present/people with factor}}{\text{disease present/people without factor}}$$

$$= \frac{A/(A + B)}{C/(C + D)}$$

$$\text{Disease Prevalence} = \frac{A + C}{A + B + C + D}$$

relative rates of developing bad eyesight, not the relative rates of carrot eating. The problem is depicted in table 10–2. We cannot move horizontally across the table to develop rates of disease for persons with and without a particular factor. The expression "A/(A + B) ÷ C/(C + D)," which would give us the relative risk, cannot be calculated because the cases and controls are not represented in relation to their prevalence in any parent population.

However, there are ways of estimating relative risk from the case-control design. By tolerating two assumptions we can come up with a serviceable substitute. First, we must hope that the control group is reasonably representative of the general population with respect to the occurrence of risk factors. Then, if the disease is relatively uncommon (as is true with most noninfectious diseases) A and C in table 10–2 will be quite small in comparison to B and D. If we simply use B and D as approximations for A + B and C + D, respectively, the problem of disease frequency no longer interferes with our calculations. The estimate of relative risk can be expressed

Table 10-2 Relative Risk Estimate in Case-Control Studies

	Cases	Controls	
Factor Present	A	B	A + B
Factor Absent	C	D	C + D

Relative Risk $= \dfrac{\text{disease present/people with factor}}{\text{disease present/people without factor}}$

But . . . $\dfrac{A}{A + B}$ and $\dfrac{C}{C + D}$ do not represent rates of disease in a population

If . . . disease has a low frequency, so that A and C are small relative to B and D in the population at large

Then . . . $\dfrac{A}{B}$ approximates $\dfrac{A}{A + B}$

and

$\dfrac{C}{D}$ approximates $\dfrac{C}{C + D}$

And . . . relative risk is approximated by $\dfrac{A/B}{C/D}$ or $\dfrac{A \times D}{B \times C}$

as A/B ÷ C/D or, in simplified form, AD/BC. This cross-product estimate of relative risk is referred to as the relative odds, odds ratio, or risk ratio. Epidemiologic purists are careful not to call this calculation a true relative risk, since the individual risk rates are approximations only.

Multiple sclerosis is an example of an uncommon disease, of uncertain etiology, that occurs with a frequency ranging from 10 to 100 cases per 100,000 population. One of many hypotheses put forth to explain this mysterious illness has been the accidental infection of man with viruses that normally reside in lower animals. One such study conducted in Vermont sent postcard questionnaires to 100 patients with multiple sclerosis and 135 control subjects asking

Table 10-3 Comparison of Multiple Sclerosis and Control Groups with Respect to Reported Exposure to Animals

	Exposure to Animal		
Animal	Multiple Sclerosis (N = 100)	Controls (N = 135)	Estimated Risk Ratio
	%		
Cats	65	57	1.4
Dogs	69	70	1.0
Rabbits	22	15	1.6
Horses	32	22	1.7
Cows	40	19	2.9
Chickens	37	14	3.6

Based on Sylwester, D. L. and Poser, C. M. [14] by permission of the *Annals of Neurology*.

for information about contact with a variety of domestic animals and household pets [14]. A summary of the findings can be seen in table 10-3. The increased frequency of exposure to animals for multiple sclerosis patients compared with controls creates risk ratios between 1 and 2 for cats, dogs, horses, and rabbits and larger risk estimates for contact with cows and chickens. Exposure to animals appears to be related to contracting multiple sclerosis. Detailed calculation of the risk ratio for chickens by the cross-product technique is shown in table 10-4.

In another study on the same subject, Cook et al. demonstrated an association between contact with pet dogs and the development of multiple sclerosis [4]. Their analysis demonstrates another commonly employed method of calculating risk ratios from case-control studies. In this study, for each patient diagnosed as having multiple sclerosis, a specific control subject was chosen who was matched by age, sex, race, and neighborhood of residence prior to the onset of symptoms in the subject. When this kind of careful matching is performed, a matched-pair analysis can be performed to calculate the risk ratio. The technique, as shown in table 10-5, involves categorizing each case-control pair by concordance or discordance with respect to the characteristic under study. In the present example,

Table 10–4   Exposure to Chickens

Exposed to Chickens	Multiple Sclerosis Cases (N = 100)	Controls (N = 135)
Yes	37	19
No	63	116

Risk Ratio $= \dfrac{A \times D}{B \times C} = \dfrac{37 \times 116}{19 \times 63} = 3.6$

Based on Sylwester, D. L. and Poser, C. M. [14] by permission of the *Annals of Neurology.*

27 multiple sclerosis patients and their matched controls owned "indoor dogs"; four other pairs were also concordant in that neither case nor control reported dog ownership. Concordance, it turns out, tells us very little. The risk ratio for matched pairs is computed by comparing discordant categories. For 12 pairs of subjects, multiple sclerosis cases reported dog ownership when controls did not, compared to only 2 pairs in which controls were exposed to dogs and multiple sclerosis cases were not. The odds or risk ratio can be directly computed as the ratio of these discordant groups, 12 ÷ 2 or 6. In other words, ownership of a dog carries a six-fold risk of multiple sclerosis.

Confidence Limits

Recalling earlier discussions of sampling and inference, it should be clear that risk ratios determined from case-control studies are based on limited samples and are subject to sampling error. Most knowledgeable investigators recognize that their data supply only a single estimate of the true relative odds or relative risk. However, based on their particular findings, they can calculate a range in which the true-risk estimate is likely to fall. This is called the confidence limits or confidence interval. When authors supply "95 percent confidence limits," it means that there is a 95 percent probability that the true value for the relative odds falls within the stated boundaries. Thus, if an odds ratio of 4.5 was found with 95 percent confidence

Table 10-5 Indoor Dog Ownership for Multiple Sclerosis Patients and Controls

		Dog Ownership for Pairs	
		Controls	
		Yes	No
Multiple	Yes	27	12
Sclerosis	No	2	4
Patients			

Risk Ratio = ratio of discordant pairs

$$= \frac{\text{case ``yes'', control ``no''}}{\text{case ``no'', control ``yes''}}$$

$$= \frac{12}{2}$$

$$= 6$$

Based on Cook, S. D. et al. [4] by permission of the *Annals of Neurology*.

limits of 2.2 and 7.8, it means that there is a 95 percent chance that the true odds lie between 2.2 and 7.8. The important feature to look for in assessing confidence limits is whether the boundaries include unity. A risk ratio of 1 means there is no association between the putative risk factor and disease. When unity lies within the confidence limits, there is a possibility that no association exists between risk factors (dog ownership) and diseases (multiple sclerosis).

Attributable Risk

Implicit in the process of identifying and defining risk factors is the hope that somehow by modifying or eliminating risk, health can be improved. How many lives could be saved if seat belts were used more? How much would morbidity be reduced by bringing everyone's blood pressure under control? What impact could we

Table 10-6 Relative Risk and Attributable Risk of Cigarette Smoking for Lung Cancer and Heart Disease

	Death Rate (per 100,000 Population)	
	From Lung Cancer	From Coronary Disease
For Heavy Smokers	223	516
For Nonsmokers	7	361
Relative Risk	$\frac{223}{7} = 32$	$\frac{516}{361} = 1.4$
Attributable Risk	$223 - 7 = 216$	$516 - 361 = 155$

Based on data from Doll, R. and Hill, A. B. [6].

have on the incidence of congenital birth defects with a national rubella-immunization campaign? Comparison of risks is useful in assessing health-care prevention and treatment programs; but where causation is best suggested by ratios of risks, health impact is addressed by examining the differences in risk rates. The attributable risk tells us the difference in rates between people who smoke, have high blood pressure, or have susceptibility to rubella and those who do not. It indicates how much of the morbidity or mortality of a disease can be attributed to the risk factor. Attributable risk quantitates the contribution risk factors make in producing disease within a population. By comparing attributable risk for different factors, we can begin to arrange informed, health-care priorities. Mortality data from the study of British doctors' smoking habits [6] demonstrates the difference between relative risk and attributable risk, as table 10-6 shows. The relative risk of lung cancer due to smoking is much greater at 32 than is the relative risk of myocardial infarction among smokers, which is only 1.4. However, heart disease is much more common than lung cancer. So, even though the relative risk associated with heart disease and smoking is small, the importance to the general health is magnified. The death rate from heart disease that can be attributed to smoking comes close to that contributed by smoking-induced lung cancer. If cigarette smoking could be eliminated, almost as many coronary-artery-disease lives could be saved as lung-cancer lives.

Risk in Perspective

The concept of risk helps quantify the likelihood of beneficial or adverse medical outcomes and guides informed decision-making, but we can sometimes lose our perspective. Announcement that a new environmental agent has been linked to cancer or that a drug may be a risk factor for birth defects raises an emotional response that occasionally obscures rational decision-making. Whenever medical decisions are made, adverse risks must be balanced against the potential benefits of the medication, surgical procedure, or immunization program. The controversy surrounding oral contraceptives is a case in point. Untoward effects of the pill have been a fertile ground for epidemiology researchers in recent years. A large number of papers have been published detailing possible associations between oral contraceptives and thromboembolic disease, stroke, heart attack, and high blood pressure. While the final answer is not in, the publicity surrounding the controversy has made many physicians and patients shy away from the contraceptives. A summary editorial of the relationship between oral contraceptives and myocardial infarction suggested that women taking the pill were 2.5 to 5 times as likely to have a fatal heart attack as women not taking the pill [9]. This is a substantial increase in risk and gives reasonable cause for alarm. However, for women 30 to 39 years of age, this increased relative risk creates an absolute rate of only 3.5 deaths per 100,000 users per year. That is a very small number. An inquisitive reader might even ask if that tiny risk is not less substantial than the risk of dying sometime in the course of pregnancy. That is an excellent question, and according to Morris [11], British data suggest that the risk of dying from pregnancy is equal to or greater than that of dying from taking oral contraceptives.

In part, the perspective problem relates to limitations in basic study designs. Because complications from oral contraceptives are rare, most studies of associated morbidity and mortality are done in a case-control fashion. This means investigators can estimate a risk ratio or relative odds but do not have a population on which to base statements of absolute or attributable risk. We lack the denominators that are vital to determine rates of people at risk. For clinicians, it is an important omission.

Practicing doctors also need to know the risk tradeoffs in prescribing medication or advising surgery. What is the risk of anaphylaxis from penicillin given to treat strep throat compared to the risk of rheumatic fever if the patient goes untreated? Is the risk of death associated with gall-bladder surgery offset by the benefits of the treatment? To make informed decisions we must have comparable data about the gains as well as the liabilities of any course of action. The risks of all complications related to oral-contraceptive use should be quantified and measured against the risks for other methods of birth control. These must then be balanced against the adverse outcomes associated with pregnancy. Data are not always available to quantify these risks. Frequently clinicians must make decisions based on insufficient information. It is important to remember however, that when the adverse relative risk of a therapy is trumpeted by the news media, the magnitude of absolute risk and benefits of the treatment should also be considered.

Let us examine another example. Reports that a serious childhood disease known as Reye syndrome may be related to salicylate ingestion have made physicians wonder if they should be advising young patients to avoid aspirin. Reye syndrome can be a devastating illness. It begins innocuously as a viral disease, such as, influenza or chicken pox. Several days into the illness, children begin to vomit, become lethargic, and progress rapidly into coma. Many cases are fatal. The etiology of the illness has been elusive, and because of its severity, researchers have eagerly tracked down any hunches that might lead to uncovering a cause and cure. The observation that aspirin use seemed high among cases of Reye syndrome led to case-control studies testing that possible association. Several of the studies indicated that aspirin may be playing a role.

Work conducted in Ohio compared histories of aspirin use for 98 children with Reye syndrome with those of a group of control children selected from the same school, classroom, or neighborhood, who had a similar antecedent illness (influenza, chicken pox, or gastroenteritis) within a week of the time the case got sick [3]. Seventy-one percent of control children had been given aspirin during their illness compared to 97 percent of the youngsters who developed Reye syndrome. This was a statistically significant difference (likely to have occurred by chance only 1 in 1,000 times) and yielded an odds ratio of 11:1. That is impressive. Children taking aspirin were 11 times more likely to contract Reye syndrome than children who were not given salicylates. The 95 percent confidence limits of this odds ratio were 2.7 to 47.5, a broad range that suggests that the true risk is substantially greater than one. Reports of studies from Michigan [3] and Arizona [13] conducted in a similar fashion produced similar results. With the collective finger pointing toward aspirin, what is a clinician to do?

The first job is to put the problem into perspective. As alarming as is Reye syndrome, it is not a common disease. We hear a great deal about it because of its suddenness and severity. Although accurate figures for the occurrence of the syndrome are not at hand, a surveillance system developed by the Centers for Disease Control (CDC) reports that in 1979, 394 cases of Reye syndrome were voluntarily reported to the center from across the nation [1]. During the five months from December 1979 through April 1980 (the months when the syndrome is most likely to occur), 304 cases were reported from 37 different states [2]. Now, while not all cases of the syndrome are reported to the CDC, the interest in the disease is great enough that underreporting is probably low. Let us assume that 50 percent of the actual cases are reported and that the true number of episodes that occurs each year is about 800. CDC reports that over 90 percent of all cases occur in children under 15 years of age. In this country in 1979 that was about 50 million children. Even if all 800 of those cases occurred in children under 15, the rate is only 1.6 per 100,000 population. Reye syndrome is a rare disease. In contrast, use of salicylates is extremely common. Over 70 percent of the control patients in the Ohio study received salicylates during the course of their minor illnesses. If we consider how many of the 50 million children in the country are likely to have minor illnesses in the course of a year for which they will receive salicylates, we realize that the vast majority of children who are exposed to aspirin will not come down with Reye syndrome. Even postulating that only 20 percent of all 50 million children had a viral infection for which they received aspirin in a single year and all cases of Reye syndrome occurred within that group, the risk of the syndrome occurring would be only 8 cases per 100,000 courses of aspirin. All this is not to deny that aspirin and Reye syndrome may be associated nor that Reye syndrome is a devastating illness, but one must weigh the risks of developing the disease against the benefits of aspirin use.

Assessing the Appropriate Outcome

Another pediatric problem that has received journal attention is infection of newborn babies with group B streptococcus. The result is a fulminant infectious disease that occurs within the first few days of life and brings with it a fatality rate of about 50 percent. Because of its early onset and rapid progression, recognition sometimes comes too late for effective therapy. Development of preventive measures has been of great interest. One study sought to remedy the problem by giving newborns an intramuscular dose of penicillin within the first hour after delivery in place of the usual topical application of tetracycline to the eyes for prevention of gonorrheal ophthalmia [12]. An experiment was devised in which the two treatments were alternated each week in a large hospital nursery. Over 18,000 infants were included in the study, 9,000 in each group. Results looked promising. Group B streptococcal infections were substantially reduced. Among infants receiving penicillin, there was only one case of early onset group B disease compared with 12 cases in the tetracycline control group. The authors found this difference was unlikely to be due to chance and concluded that the prophylaxis was effective in reducing group B streptococcal disease.

Unfortunately, the penicillin prophylaxis program was accompanied by an increase in disease caused by penicillin-resistant bacteria. These infections caused greater mortality than did group B streptococcal infections. The overall death rate in penicillin-treated babies was 12, for a rate of 1.3 per 1,000 births, compared with only 5 deaths (0.5 per 1,000) in the tetracycline control group. This information gives a slightly different flavor to the conclusions. If the goal of penicillin prophylaxis is to reduce deaths due to nursery infections, the program appears less than successful.

Summary

Statements of risk help us quantify the dangers of the environment; they serve as guides to prognosis and measures of potential effectiveness of health-intervention activities. Relative risk is useful for testing hypotheses about etiologic association. Attributable risk provides a population perspective to assess the impact of changing risk factors on the general health.

Risk statements must be kept in perspective. Estimates of relative risk are derived from samples and, like any other samples, are prone to error. Authors who place confidence limits around their risk estimates provide readers with helpful information about the true likelihood that a factor is related to disease. Caution must be exercised in interpreting relative risk estimates without information about the absolute magnitude of risk. When risk factors are common as with use of tampons, birth-control pills, or aspirin, and adverse outcomes, such as, toxic-shock syndrome, heart attack or Reye syndrome are uncommon, risks must be balanced against benefits. Before new treatments are advocated or established medications blacklisted, the overall health impact must be considered.

References

1. CENTER FOR DISEASE CONTROL. Annual summary 1979: Reported morbidity and mortality in the United States. *Morbidity Mortality Weekly Rep.* 28:99, 1979.

2. CENTER FOR DISEASE CONTROL. Follow-up on Reye syndrome—United States. *Morbidity Mortality Weekly Rep.* 29:321–322, 1980.

3. CENTER FOR DISEASE CONTROL. Reye syndrome—Ohio, Michigan. *Morbidity Mortality Weekly Rep.* 29:532–539, 1980.

4. COOK, S. D., NATELSON, B. H., LEVIN, B. E., CHAVIS, P. S., AND DOWLING, P. C. Further evidence of a possible association between house dogs and multiple sclerosis. *Ann. Neurol.* 3:141–143, 1978.

5. DAVIS, J. P., CHESNEY, P. J., WAND, P. J., LAVENTURE, M., ET AL. Toxic-shock syndrome: Epidemiologic features, recurrence, risk factors, and prevention. *N. Engl. J. Med.* 303:1429–1435, 1980.

6. DOLL, R. AND HILL, A. B. Mortality in relation to smoking: Ten

years' observations of British doctors. *Brit. Med. J.* 1:1399–1410, 1460–1467, 1964.

7. FRIEDMANN, E., KATCHER, A. H., LYNCH, J. J., AND THOMAS, S. A. Animal companions and one-year survival after discharge from a coronary care unit. *Public Health Rep.* 95:.307–312, 1980.

8. HAILE, C. A. Chloramphenicol toxicity. *Southern Med. J.* 70:479–480, 1977.

9. HENNEKENS, C. H. AND MACMAHON, B. Oral contraceptives and myocardial infarction. *N. Engl. J. Med.* 296:1166–1167, 1977.

10. JENKINS, C. D., ROSENMAN, R. H., AND ZYZANSKI, S. J. Prediction of clinical coronary heart disease by a test for the coronary-prone behavior pattern. *N. Engl. J. Med.* 290:1271–1275, 1974.

11. MORRIS, J. N. *Uses of Epidemiology.* 3rd Edition. Edinburgh: Churchill Livingstone, 1975.

12. SEIGEL, J. D., MCCRACKEN, G. H., THRELKELD, N., MILVENAN, B., AND ROSENFELD, C. R. Single-dose penicillin prophylaxis against neonatal Group B streptococcal infections: A controlled trial in 18,738 newborn infants. *N. Engl. J. Med.* 303:769–775, 1980.

13. STARKO, K. M., RAY, G. G., DOMINQUEZ, L. B., STROMBERG, W. L., AND WOODALL, D. F. Reye's syndrome and salicylate use. *Pediatrics* 66:859–864, 1980.

14. SYLWESTER, D. L. AND POSER, C. M. The association of multiple sclerosis with domestic animals and household pets. *Ann. Neurol.* 2:207–208, 1979.

ELEVEN

Interpretation: Causes

> *. . . and now remains that we find out the cause of this effect.*
> *Or rather say the cause of this defect. For this effect defective*
> *comes by cause . . .*
> —Hamlet, *Act II, Scene II*

Poor Polonius, a tracker of truth, trapped in his own logical snares. He never does ferret out the cause of Hamlet's madness. Is it due to unrequited love, a father's death, or Denmark's melancholy climate? Polonius fails to find out. Indeed, he dies midway through the investigation, undone by his own hazardous techniques of study design.

Chasing after causes in medical studies is difficult though not usually terminal business. Up to now we have minced about with phrases such as "associated with," "linked to," and "related to." We have avoided dogmatic statements of causation, such as, oral contraceptives cause vascular complications, aspirin is the etiology behind Reye syndrome, or eating lead paint is responsible for lower IQs among children. We have been reluctant to totally accept that vitamin C wards off colds or that birthing rooms are responsible for decreased problems in childbirth. Even when we think we have pinpointed the guilty party, the possibility remains that some unsuspected risk factor is actually causing the disease or an unappreciated cointervention is responsible for the treatment effect. In this chapter, we will look for ways to decide whether the associations found in studies merit consideration as causes, and note some ways in which investigators deal with multiple potential explanations for the outcomes they observe.

Confounding

In Chapter 3, matching was discussed as a method of handling confusing or confounding factors in case-control studies. Confounding occurred when factors that related to both the characteristic under scrutiny and the outcome appeared as competing explanations. The example we used was the apparent etiologic relationship between cigar smoking and baldness; an association that was confused or confounded by age. The data from this study appear in table 11–1. We select 50 bald men to represent the cases and find over one-half of them are cigar smokers. In the control group, only 8 of 50 subjects chosen admit to the habit. Using the cross-product estimation for the risk ratio, we see that there is a six-fold $[(27 \times 42)/(23 \times 8) = 1134/184 = 6.2]$ risk of baldness associated with cigar smoking. However, in examining the data we realize that the ages of men in the groups being compared is dissimilar. Our bald subjects average 52 years of age compared with a mean age of 24 years for controls. Quite a disparity! Since we know that increasing age is related both to cigar smoking and to loss of hair we have a problem with confounding. Matching on age, that is, selecting only control subjects whose age is within several years of the cases is one way of *controlling* the effects of age. When we redo our experiment, choosing only cases and controls who are between the ages of 40 and 45 years, the hypothetical results appear as in table 11–2. Now the rates of cigar smoking are similar for cases and control, that is, about 40 percent. The risk ratio, as calculated by the cross-products

Table 11–1   Rate of Cigar Smoking for Bald Men Compared with Controls

		Baldness		
		Yes (cases)	No (controls)	
Cigar Smoking	Yes	27	8	
	No	23	42	
		50	50	100

$$\text{Relative odds} = \frac{27 \times 42}{23 \times 8} = \frac{1134}{184} = 6.2$$

Table 11-2 Rate of Cigar Smoking for Bald Men 40 to 45 Years Old Compared with Age-Matched Controls

		Baldness		
		Yes (cases)	No (controls)	
Cigar Smoking	Yes	21	23	
	No	29	27	
		50	50	100

$$\text{Relative odds} = \frac{21 \times 27}{29 \times 23} = \frac{567}{667} = .85$$

estimate, is very close to one. There is no longer an association between smoking and hair loss. Confounding has been eliminated.

Confounding is the epidemiologist's eternal triangle. Any time a risk factor, patient characteristic, or intervention appears to be causing a disease, side effect, or outcome, the relationship needs to be challenged. Are we seeing cause and effect, or is a confounding factor exerting its unappreciated influence? The problem is schematized in figure 11-1. It is important to remember that to be a confounding variable, a factor must be related both to the outcome or effect and to the putative cause.

Let us look at some other examples. The apparent protective effect that animal companions afforded heart-attack victims [8] would seem a situation ripe for confounding. Recall that pet owners had a better than six-fold greater likelihood of survival in the first year following discharge from a coronary-care unit than patients who were without animal companions. The authors report that their findings are consistent with the hypothesis that social affiliation and companionship have important, positive health benefits. Are there other equally plausible explanations? Are there other attributes pet owners possess that might contribute to a more favorable outlook for survival after heart attack? Several possibilities come to mind. Perhaps people who tolerate pets possess more easy-going personalities and less coronary-prone, aggressive behavior that predisposes to future cardiac problems. Or perhaps because pets require attention and care,

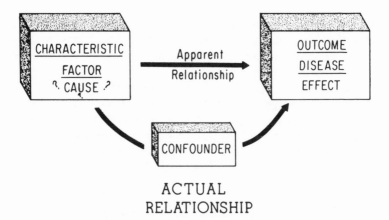

ACTUAL
RELATIONSHIP

Figure 11-1. *The confounding triangle.*

pet owners tend to be younger and more active than nonowners and thus more likely to survive.

In one article about the possible relationship between salicylate use and the development of Reye syndrome [18], the potential for confounding is substantial. Seven patients who developed Reye syndrome after apparently minor illnesses were compared with 16 sex-matched classmates who were also mildly ill about the same time. So far, so good. The authors have already done some basic matching (age, sex, season, school) to try to ensure comparability between the two groups. After interviewing the parents of the 23 children, investigators discovered that all 7 of the patients with Reye syndrome received aspirin compared with only 8 of the 16 control subjects. This difference did not appear to be due to chance (p < .05) and suggests a relationship between aspirin ingestion and the development of the disease. Could other factors play a role? An obvious question would be whether the mild illnesses that the children experienced were similar for cases and controls. Aspirin may have been given preferentially to children who had more severe prodromal illness and is not the causative agent but a marker for disease severity.

In fact, there is evidence in the data to suggest that cases and controls had different types of illness. All 5 of the 7 cases whose temperatures were taken had fevers greater than 38.3°C. Temperatures this high were observed in only 4 of the 16 control subjects, however. Since a principal indication for aspirin administration is fever, there is a reasonable possibility that the drug is only second-arily associated with the development of Reye syndrome because it was given to the sicker children.

Confounding factors are always in the shadows, ready to cast doubt on the interpretation of studies. The apparent link between lead-paint ingestion and low IQ may be confounded by poor social environment, which is related both to intellectual underachievement and accessability to lead paint. The improved perinatal outcomes of women utilizing the alternative birthing center may not be due to the innovative facility but to the improved outcomes that come with the healthier, better educated, more highly motivated volunteers who select the birthing center option. With confounding a ubiquitous danger, savvy authors will make some effort to deal with these po-tential alternative explanations.

Methods of Dealing With Confounding

Confounding may be attacked either in the design of the study or during analysis. Matching and stratifying are techniques used in the design stage. Matching, as discussed in Chapter 3, is generally utilized in observational studies. Comparison subjects are selected who share specific similarities (age, weight, race, sex) with the cases. Matched characteristics are eliminated as competing ex-planations of the disease. In experimental designs, stratification prior to allocation serves a similar purpose. The controlled trial comparing Leboyer childbirth to conventional delivery was susceptible to con-founding [15]. Unequal (chance) distribution of obstetrical risk fac-tors among women assigned to the two methods could have created the appearance of disparate outcomes. The threat was controlled when random allocation was performed only after subjects had been rated and stratified by obstetrical risk.

Matching or stratifying before the fact is not always practical. Investigators may not be able to choose ideal controls or may not anticipate potential confounding factors in advance. Techniques are available for controlling the effects of confounding during the analysis of data. Two methods that readers will commonly encounter are control tables and multivariate analysis.

Control Tables

The control-table method is stratification ex post facto. Rather than arranging subjects by age groups, smoking habits or blood-pressure levels as the study design is being created, results are calculated within specified subdivisions.

An example of a confounding relationship that has perplexed researchers for a number of years is the possible link between sugar consumption and heart disease. Back in the early 1960s, Yudkin and Roddy postulated that increased intake of sucrose might lead to coronary artery disease [21]. In a case-control study they compared 20 subjects recovering from acute myocardial infarctions with 25 controls who were either healthy or were patients on an orthopedic ward. Mean sugar intake for the two groups differed considerably as shown in table 11-3. Heart disease patients reported consuming almost twice as much sugar as controls. These were provocative findings and stimulated other researchers to test the hypothesis [3,5,7]. In the course of this subsequent work, it became apparent that individuals who consumed high amounts of sugar had other habits that might be related to heart disease. They consumed substantial amounts of coffee and tea, and they smoked more. While the issue is still not resolved to everyone's satisfaction, the relationship of smoking, which most researchers agree is a risk factor for heart disease, to sugar consumption has created a confounding problem. For purposes of illustration, let us use some hypothetical data to see how this confounding might work.

Yudkin's figures show that heart disease patients consume an average of 132 grams of sugar per day compared with 77 grams daily for controls. If, however, people who eat more sugar also smoke

Table 11-3 Mean Daily Sugar Consumption for 20 Patients with Heart Disease and 25 Control Subjects

	Sugar Consumption (grams/day)
Heart-Disease Patients (N = 20)	132
Control Subjects (N = 25)	77

Based on data from Yudkin, J. and Roddy, J. [21] by permission.

Table 11–4 Mean Daily Sugar Consumption for 20 Patients with Heart Disease and 25 Control Subjects (Controlled for Smoking)

	Sugar Consumption (grams/day)
Heart-Disease Patients (N = 20)	132
Smokers (N = 16)	152
Nonsmokers (N = 4)	50
Control Subjects (N = 25)	77
Smokers (N = 7)	148
Nonsmokers (N = 18)	50

more, and smokers are apportioned differently among cases and controls, the results might appear as in table 11–4. The overall averages reflect the apparent association; but by evaluating sugar intake within subgroups of smoking and nonsmoking subjects, the effects of smoking are controlled. Once this is done, the relationship between sugar consumption and heart disease disappears. Mean sugar consumption for heart-disease patients who smoke is almost identical to that of smoking control patients. Likewise, nonsmokers consume only 50 grams of sucrose per day regardless of whether or not they have heart disease. Smoking is related to heart disease; sucrose intake is not. It is apparent, however, that for the relationship between sucrose and heart disease to completely disappear, smokers must be very unevenly distributed. Sixteen of the 20 heart-attack patients must be smokers compared with only 7 of the 25 controls to achieve the results that were obtained.

Frequently, a confounding factor exerts an influence on results but is not entirely responsible for findings. When Elwood et al. attempted to replicate Yudkin's work, they found that smoking indeed confounded the relationship between sugar consumption and heart disease, but that even when smoking was controlled, a small residual relationship remained [7]. Table 11–5 depicts two different ways our hypothetical data can be displayed. Both formats are encountered in medical articles and are referred to as control tables. Table 11–5b looks just like the two-by-two tables we used before to categorize subjects by diseases and characteristics, but it is a bit more

Table 11–5   Mean Daily Sugar Consumption for 20 Patients with Heart Disease and 25 Control Subjects (Controlled for Smoking)

	Sugar Consumption (grams/day)
(a)	
Heart-Disease Patients (N = 20)	132
Smokers (N = 12)	152
Nonsmokers (N = 8)	101
Control Subjects (N = 25)	77
Smokers (N = 10)	118
Nonsmokers (N = 15)	50

(b)

Sugar Consumption (grams/day)

	Heart Disease	Controls
Smokers	152 (N = 12)	118 (N = 10)
Nonsmokers	101 (N = 8)	50 (N = 15)

complex. It shows the relationship between three rather than two variables. The figures in each box no longer represent the number of subjects, they portray an attribute of the subjects—in this case, mean daily sugar consumption. Reading the rows of the control table, comparing smokers with nonsmokers, we find that regardless of whether subjects have heart disease or not, smokers have higher sugar consumption (152 grams per day compared with 101 grams per day, 118 grams per day compared with 50 grams per day). Inspecting the columns, we see that patients with heart disease also consume more sugar than patients without heart disease in both the smoking and the nonsmoking groups. The conclusion to be drawn from this table is that the relationship between sugar consumption and heart disease is in fact confounded by smoking. But when the effect of smoking is held constant, the association between sucrose consumption and heart disease remains. Both smoking and sugar are related to heart problems.

Multivariate Analysis

Control tables are dandy for handling confounding variables when only one or two of the confusing factors are around. However, in many situations a number of explanations are competing for causation credit. Human behavior is complex business. Heart disease has been linked to age, diet, personality type, blood pressure, cigarette smoking, and cholesterol levels. Pregnancy outcome has been shown to be related to maternal age, race, socioeconomic status, parity, and marital status to mention a few. Many of these causal factors are interrelated. When it comes time to sort out just what is responsible for an outcome or effect, simple control tables are not up to the task. By the time we have tried to compare the sugar consumption of subjects who are of the same sex, same age, smoke the same amount, have similar cholesterol levels, and have the same range of blood pressure, life has become exceedingly complex. The more factors we control in a data analysis, the smaller the number of subjects becomes in each subdivision and the larger samples must be to avoid making incorrect inferences.

Fortunately, there are some statistical techniques available that can help. These mathematical manipulations fall under the general rubric of multivariate analyses and include regression analysis, discriminant analysis, general linear models, and several more. They are not the kind of pencil and paper calculations that most clinicians find useful to master, but it is worth noting how they aid in the interpretation of an article. Essentially, multivariate techniques are used when investigators wish to sort through a tangle of interrelated variables to learn which are contributing to the effect or outcome.

When the relationship between survival after discharge from the coronary-care unit and pet ownership was being explored, the authors realized that a number of factors govern prognosis following heart attack [8]. Among the most important of these are the subject's age and the complications surrounding the cardiac event. In an attempt to decide just where pets fit into this complex prognostic scheme, the investigators employed a discriminant function analysis to control for physiological severity, age, mood, support, and social isolation. They did so to corral variables that might be related both to heart disease and pet ownership. Although it turns out that having a pet is not nearly so potent a predictor of survival as the physiological severity of the initial heart attack, pets made a contribution to outcome that was independent of the other factors considered.

A note of caution, however. Interpreting the results of multivariate analyses requires the same keep-your-wits-about-you approach as assessing statistical significance. The fact that the discriminant function analysis showed pet ownership played a statistically significant role in survival does not necessarily mean that discharge orders for cardiac patients should include advice to purchase a dog or cat. Results of this particular study indicate that only 2.5 percent of the total variance is explained by pet ownership. This means that in the multivariate mathematical model used to predict survival, pet ownership has only a small predictive role.

One last point. Simply using sophisticated, multivariate techniques to sort out multiple possible explanations of a phenomenon does not guarantee success. The authors of the pet study postulate that pet ownership is directly linked to survival by the protective effects of companionship. We need not be convinced. Pet ownership may still be a proxy for some unidentified attributes shared by people who will have more favorable outcomes following heart attack. The discriminant analysis may not have addressed these factors. The advice offered for interpreting statistical significance is worth reiterating. If authors' conclusions lack plausibility, fancy statistical techniques will not a silk purse make.

Making Associations into Causes

Tracking causes more often takes us through a labyrinth of tangled streets than down a straight path. When we have stripped away confounders and convinced ourselves that an exposure factor or intervention is directly and independently linked to a disease or outcome, we still may not have a complete picture. Even if we are convinced that Reye syndrome is directly related to aspirin ingestion, what is the exact cause of the illness? Does the drug act as a direct liver toxin? Why do only a handful of children that take aspirin contract the disease? Is the illness a response to a mix of factors including host susceptibility, concurrent viral illness, and the drug? The causes of even seemingly straightforward infectious diseases are surprisingly complex. It is overly simple, for example, to say that tuberculosis is caused by the tubercle bacillus. While the infecting organism must be present for tuberculosis to occur, only 10 percent to 15 percent of individuals that are infected with the germ ever

Table 11-6   Features of Associations That Support Causation

1. The strength of the association
2. Consistency of observed evidence
3. Specificity of the relationship
4. Temporality of relationship
5. The biological gradient of dose-response
6. Biological plausibility
7. Coherence of the evidence
8. Experimental confirmation
9. Reasoning by analogy

Based on Hill, A. B. [10].

develop active tuberculosis. The bacillus is a necessary but not a sufficient cause for the illness. Host resistance, nutritional status, social isolation, and adaptability to stress also play a role. Discussions of cause can rapidly become metaphysical as well as biological. For readers who are interested in detailed discussions of the subject, some thought-provoking reviews are available [17,19].

For practical purposes, most clinicians have a threshold at which the evidence for etiology is strong enough to elicit action. John Snow reportedly dismantled the Broad Street pump to curtail the cholera that was raging in mid-19th century London when he was convinced of the causal role that water played in the epidemic; but his action preceded the identification of the cholera vibrio, which most would consider the cause of cholera, by several decades.

There are several practical hints that clinician readers can use to help decide whether the associations they read about are causal enough to precipitate action. Hill has published a classic essay on causation [10]. He speaks of nine features of relationships that are useful in constructing a case for causation. These are summarized in table 11-6. At the risk of repetition, it is worth elaborating on some of these points in more detail.

Strength of the Association

One bit of evidence that tips the association balance toward causality is the strength of the association. When the relative risk or relative odds are high, the argument for cause gains support. The hackneyed but potent example used to illustrate the point is the association between cigarette smoking and lung cancer. Here, risk ratios as high as 30 to 1 have been found. The statement that a heavy cigarette user is 30 times more likely to contract lung cancer than a nonsmoker is difficult to ignore. In the reserpine-breast cancer story, on the other hand, the case for causation is weakened when the magnitude of risk is assessed. Some early studies linking the medication with the cancer boasted overall risk ratios of only 1.2–3.5 to 1 [4,9,13], a less impressive relationship.

Dose-Response Relationship

Anytime a risk factor comes in doses or gradients of exposure, it is reasonable to expect that the risk of disease should increase with higher levels of exposure. Again, cigarette smoking and lung cancer provide the perfect example as the work of Doll and Hill shows [6] (see figure 11–2). The more cigarettes people smoke, the more death rates from cancer go up and that implies causality.

This same type of evidence has been used to strengthen the ties between postmenopausal use of estrogens and development of endometrial cancer. Weiss et al. have shown that the risk of cancer is greater in women who have taken high-estrogen-content medication than for those who have consumed a lesser amount [20]. Table 11–7 demonstrates the rise in relative risk associated with increasing daily dosage. On the other hand, the lack of a biologic gradient or dose-response relationship where one might expect it should give pause for thought. Several studies have attempted to establish a causal relationship between ingestion of artificial sweeteners and development of bladder cancer [11,12,14]. Findings have been inconsistent. Among the pieces of puzzle that have failed to fit together are those showing increased risk of cancer as intake of artificial sweeteners increases. Table 11–8 displays the data from one case-control study comparing estimates of intake of artificial sweeteners in patients with bladder cancer and controls [12]. Although there is some indication that increasing intake of sweeteners is associated with increased risk of cancer in men, the trend is actually reversed for women.

Biological Plausibility

To make a convincing argument for causation, the associations developed in medical studies should make biological sense. This means they should be consistent with information avail-

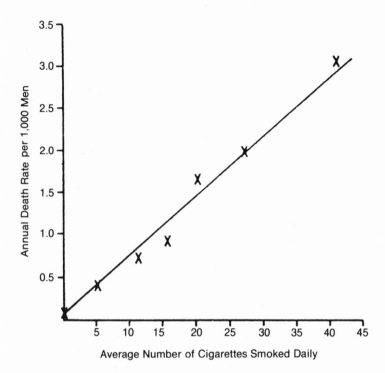

Figure 11-2. Annual death rate per 1,000 men by average number of cigarettes smoked daily. (From Doll, R. and Hill, A. B. [6] with permission.)

able from the related worlds of physiology, pharmacology, and anatomy. One argument that strengthens the case for estrogens as a cause for endometrial cancer has been the demonstration of concordance between the duration of exposure and development of disease. What we know of neoplasia suggests that cancers are not triggered immediately on exposure to a carcinogen but develop after a latent period. We would expect that women exposed to estrogens would contract the neoplasm only some years after initial exposure. Table 11-9 depicts the increasing relative risk associated with the length of time since women were first exposed to estrogens. Women with less than three years on the medication have essentially no increased risk of cancer.

Results are sometimes called into question because of apparent gaps in biological plausibility. Interpretation of data from the anturane reinfarction trial have been complicated by findings that seem

Table 11–7 Menopausal Estrogen Use in Women with Endometrial Cancer and Controls According to Average Daily Dosage

Average Dosage mg/day	% of Subjects		Relative Risk	95% Confidence Interval
	Endometrial Cancer (N = 309)	Control (N = 272)		
Never Used	20	63	1.0	. . . .
≤ 0.5	5	7	2.5	1.1—5.3
0.6—1.2	32	12	8.8	5.0—12.7
≥ 1.25	44	18	7.6	5.0—11.6

From Weiss, N. S. et al. [20] by permission of *JAMA* 242:261–264, 1979. Copyright © 1979, American Medical Association.

inconsistent with the properties of the drug under study [1]. The purpose of this large controlled trial was to see if sulfinpyrazone, a drug that inhibits platelet aggregation, would prove useful in preventing death among patients recovering from heart attack. This multicenter study compared mortality rates of over 1,500 patients who had suffered myocardial infarction and were randomized to receive either sulfinpyrazone or placebo. After 24 months of follow-up, the sulfinpyrazone group had experienced approximately 32 percent less cardiac mortality than placebo-treated patients, a finding that "borders on conventional levels of statistical significance (p = 0.058)."

However, close inspection of the results revealed that this difference was due almost entirely to prevention of sudden death (presumably due to arrhythmias) rather than recurrent myocardial

Table 11–8 Relative Risk of Bladder Cancer by Level of Exposure to Artificial Sweeteners

Relative Risk	Level of Exposure		
	Low	Medium	High
Men	1.1	1.4	1.0
Women	1.2	0.7	0.7

Adapted from Kessler, I. I., and Clark, J. P. [12] by permission.

Table 11-9 Menopausal Estrogen Use in Women with Endometrial Cancer and Controls According to Time Since First Use

Average Dosage mg/day	% of Subjects		Relative Risk	95% Confidence Interval
	Endometrial Cancer (N = 281)	Control (N = 251)		
Never used	22	68	1.0	. . . .
1—2	2	4	1.2	0.4— 3.7
3—4	7	4	5.4	2.5—11.5
5—7	14	9	4.7	2.6— 8.4
8—10	19	6	11.7	6.2—21.8
11—14	20	3	24.2	11.8—49.4
15—19	13	4	10.2	5.3—20.0
⩾ 20	4	1	8.3	2.8—24.5

From Weiss, N. S. et al. [20] by permission of *JAMA* 242:261–264, 1979. Copyright © 1979, American Medical Association.

infarction. In fact, reinfarction rates for the two groups were identical. This was an unexpected finding, and it does not fit with the postulated beneficial effect of sulfinpyrazone. The drug is supposed to prevent platelet aggregation and subsequent reinfarction, not prevent arrhythmias. So while the medication appears to work, it works for the wrong reasons. Perhaps further research will demonstrate a perfectly plausible explanation for these seemingly implausible results. In the meantime, one cannot help but withhold unbridled enthusiasm for sulfinpyrazone until the mechanism by which it obtains its protective effects is clarified.

Consistency

Evidence ought to hang together in a consistent manner, both within the confines of a study and from one study to another. An additional mark against the possible causal relationship between artificial sweeteners and bladder cancer is made by the inconsistency of the data. While weak associations have been noted between sweeteners and cancer in some of the case-control studies undertaken [11,14], significant findings have been limited to subgroups of the population. In one early study, investigators found an increased risk of 1.6 for bladder neoplasms in men who ingested sugar substitutes [11]. However, this relationship was not seen for women, who had a risk of less than one (0.6). In a more recent article [14], the results were reversed. The slight excess risk that could be attributed to artificial sweeteners was demonstrated only for women and not for men (relative risks of 1.6 and 0.8, respectively). This inconsistency, together with the low strength of association that was found, weakens the case for cause.

If an association between a factor and a disease is demonstrated time and time again through a number of studies that utilize different populations and different study techniques, the argument for causation is improved. Once more the smoking/lung cancer story serves as a paradigm. The evidence for causation just keeps growing. The association is demonstrated in case-control studies in which patients with lung cancer admit to substantially higher use of cigarettes than controls. It is also seen in follow-up studies, such as those of British doctors conducted by Doll and Hill [6]. The evidence connecting reserpine and breast cancer, on the other hand, is weakened by the criterion of consistency. The initial flurry of articles that connected the medication with breast carcinoma were case-control designs performed on hospitalized populations [2,4,9]. When the later community-based studies were reported, [13,16], the role of reserpine in producing breast cancer faded.

Summary

The search for causation is always under the ominous shadow of confounding factors. Characteristics that seem directly related to outcomes or diseases may be incorrectly identified as causal because of linkages with intermediary, confounding variables. Careful readers should ask:

1. Have the authors addressed the possibility that confounding factors are responsible for the effects they have observed?

2. Have steps been taken to control confounding? Were matching or stratification strategies employed when the study design was created, or have multivariate techniques or control tables been employed in the analysis?

3. If authors have supplied evidence that potentially causal factors are not confounded, what additional evidence is there to suggest causality? Does evidence of the strength of the association, the biological plausibility, the consistency, and the dose-response relationship make a convincing case?

References

1. ANTURANE REINFARCTION TRIAL RESEARCH GROUP. Sulfin-pyrazone in the prevention of sudden death after myocardial infarction. *N. Engl. J. Med.* 302:250–256, 1980.

2. ARMSTRONG, B., STEVENS, N., AND DOLL, R. Retrospective study of the association between use of rauwolfia derivatives and breast cancer in English women. *Lancet* 2:672–675, 1974.

3. BENNETT, A. E., DOLL, R., AND HOWELL, R. W. Sugar consumption and cigarette smoking. *Lancet* 1:1011–1014, 1970.

4. BOSTON COLLABORATIVE DRUG PROGRAM. Reserpine and breast cancer. *Lancet* 2:669–671, 1974.

5. BURNS-COX, C. J., DOLL, R., AND BALL, K. P. Sugar intake and myocardial infarction. *Brit. Heart J.* 31:485–490, 1969.

6. DOLL, R. AND HILL, A. B. Mortality in relation to smoking: Ten years' observations of British doctors. *Brit. Med. J.* 1:1399–1410, 1964.

7. ELWOOD, P. C., WATERS, W. E., MOORE, S., AND SWEETNAM, P. Sucrose consumption and ischemic heart disease in the community. *Lancet* 1:1014–1016, 1970.

8. FRIEDMANN, E., KATCHER, A. H., LYNCH, J. J., AND THOMAS, S. A. Animal companions and one-year survival of patients after discharge from a coronary care unit. *Public Health Rep.* 95:307–312, 1980.

9. HEINONEN, O. P., SHAPIRO, S., TUONIMEN, L., AND TURUNEN, M. I. Reserpine use in relation to breast cancer. *Lancet* 2:675–677, 1974.

10. HILL, A. B. *Principles of Medical Statistics.* New York: Oxford University Press, 1971.

11. HOWE, G. R., BURCH, J. D., MILLER, A. B., ET AL. Artificial sweeteners and human bladder cancer. *Lancet* 2:578–581, 1977.

12. KESSLER, I. I. AND CLARK, J. P. Saccharin, cyclamate, and human bladder cancer. No evidence of an association. *JAMA* 240:349–355, 1978.

13. MACK, T. M., HENDERSON, B. E., GERKINS, V. R., ARTHUR, M., BAPTISTA, J., AND PIKE, M. C. Reserpine and breast cancer in a retirement community. *N. Engl. J. Med.* 292:1366–1371, 1975.

14. MORRISON, A. S. AND BURING, J. E. Artificial sweeteners and cancer of the lower urinary tract. *N. Engl. J. Med.* 302:537–541, 1980.

15. NELSON, N. M., ENKIN, M. W., SAIGAL, S., BENNETT, K. J., MILNER, R., AND SACKETT, D. L. A randomized clinical trial of the Leboyer approach to childbirth. *N. Engl. J. Med.* 302:655–660, 1980.

16. O'FALLON, W. M., LABARTHE, D. R., AND KURLAND, L. T. Rauwolfia derivatives and breast cancer. A case-control study in Olmstead County, Minnesota. *Lancet* 2:292–296, 1975.

17. ROTHMAN, K. J. Causes. *Am. J. Epidemiol.* 104:587–592, 1976.

18. STARKO, K. M., RAY, C. G., DOMINGUEZ, L. B., STROMBERG, W. L., AND WOODALL, D. F. Reye's syndrome and salicylate use. *Pediatrics* 66:859–864, 1980.

19. SUSSER, M. *Causal Thinking in the Health Sciences: Concepts and Strategies of Epidemiology.* New York: Oxford University Press, 1973.

20. WEISS, N. S., SZEKELY, D. R., ENGLISH, D. R., AND SCHWEID, A. I. Endometrial cancer in relation to patterns of menopausal estrogen use. *JAMA* 242:261–264, 1979.

21. YUDKIN, J. AND RODDY, J. Levels of dietary sucrose in patients with occlusive atherosclerotic disease. *Lancet* 2:6–8, 1964.

TWELVE

A Final Word

> *"When I use a word," Humpty Dumpty said in a rather scornful tone, "it means just what I choose it to mean—neither more nor less."*
>
> *"The question is," said Alice, "whether you can make words mean so many different things."*
>
> *"The question is," said Humpty Dumpty, "which is to be master—that's all."*
>
> —*Lewis Carroll,* Through the Looking Glass

As promised, we have worked our way through the major structure of a medical article. We have sampled study designs and their strengths and weaknesses, looked at the way data are collected and at some biases that creep into that activity, and devoted considerable energy to critically evaluating the way results are presented and analyzed. Along the way we discovered many pitfalls that plague medical studies and journal articles. We uncovered biases that occur because of selective recall, loss to follow-up, and poor sampling techniques. We saw the untoward effects of observer bias, the havoc wreaked by confounding factors, and the confusion created by misinterpretation of normal distributions and statistical significance.

Hopefully, we have developed some critical cutlery by learning something of random allocation, stratification, control tables, and confidence limits. In this last chapter the accent will be on mobilizing the concepts of the previous pages into a final assessment of the value of an article. After all is said and done, is the information contained within the glossy pages worth retaining? Is it information that will change practice habits or improve patient care? Is the message the authors are conveying worth our continued consideration?

It has been mentioned before but is worth repeating that medical studies are rarely free from blemish. With our sharpened critical awareness, it is possible to find a tender spot in almost any article. The trick is to put skills to work in a constructive manner, balance the good points and the flaws, and decide upon a report's overall merit. Skills in critical analysis are easily abused. Without temperance, skepticism can degenerate to nihilism. That nets very little. On the other hand, as we pass from a thorough review of a study's methodology, through a careful evaluation of the collection of data and presentation of results, to the authors' discussion, we need to have confidence in our own abilities as critical reviewers. As authors put forth their interpretation and discuss the meaning of their work, we have every right to exercise our hard-earned opinions. If cynicism is a danger, so is self-effacement. Too often readers are willing to accept the judgment of medical writers and editors over their own reactions. Under intimidation by the experts, common sense is put aside. That is a mistake. The question, as Humpty Dumpty puts to Alice, is "which is to be master?"

Clarity

Most of us have had the unsettling experience of reading an article once and then a second time only to be left with the unhappy realization that we had no idea what the author was trying to say. Most often we take this to heart as a personal shortcoming, a void in our education or basic intellect that we fail to grasp the message. Rarely do we consider that it may be the writer's rather than the reader's deficiency. Medical articles are not always clearly written. Crichton has assailed medical writers for obfuscation, for camouflaging their communication in awkward prose and unnecessary complexity [2]. He says the effect of this bad writing is to:

> make medical prose as dense, impressive and forbidding as possible . . . the stance of authors seems designed to astound and mystify the reader with a dazzling display of knowledge and scientific accumen . . . what they (authors) are communicating is their profound *scientific-ness,* not whatever the title of their paper may be. [2]

Crichton's accusations that medical writers deliberately write obscurely to conceal thin papers and appear scientifically profound may smack of hyperbole, but there are seeds of truth. There is even some objective evidence to support Crichton's claims that medical minds can mistake bombast for wisdom. Researchers interested in medical-student evaluations conducted several experiments assessing what has become known as the Doctor Fox effect [8]. In these studies, an actor was trained to lecture to medical students in a manner that would seduce them into feeling "satisfied that they had learned despite the presentation of irrelevant, conflicting, and meaningless content." The actor, dubbed "Dr. Fox," delivered his lectures with style, humor, and verve. They were, however, fillled with "double talk, neologisms, non sequiturs, and contradictory statements." Students rating Dr. Fox gave his lectures highest marks in both style and content.

Impressed by the effects of the Dr. Fox experiment, Armstrong applied the principle to professional journals [1]. To test the hypothesis that "researchers who want to impress their colleagues . . . write less intelligible papers," he asked twenty business-school faculty members to rate ten management journals according to journal prestige. The readability of each journal was then assessed by applying a reading ease test to sample articles. The test determined readability by sentence length and the number of syllables for each 100 words. Sure enough, there was a positive correlation between wordy, polysyllabic sentences and the estimated prestige. Because it might be argued that the content of the high-tone journals is more sophisticated and thus requires more elaborate prose, Armstrong added a second part to his experiment. He took concluding paragraphs from several articles and rewrote them, altering the readability but not the content. He sent these to another group of faculty members, asking them to rate the competency of the articles, based on the samples provided. Again, pedantry triumphed. Obscure writing tended to be rated higher in competence than simple, straightforward prose.

Although it may be unfair to generalize from management journals to medical writing, there is a message in this for medical readers. Clarity is the author's responsibility. If convoluted sentences and hazy verbiage obscure meaning, it's the writer's fault. Readers need to shake off the notion that their intellectual inadequacies are to blame when they have difficulty understanding a study. By the time most of us reach the stage where medical articles are appropriate reading, we are smart enough to understand them.

Apologies, Tentative Conclusions, Self-Criticism, and the Like

It is interesting to see how authors critique their own work in the discussion and conclusion sections of articles. Some authors are supremely certain of their results, others are overly modest. Blustering self-confidence invites close scrutiny when the author "doth protest too much." Results that are "truly obvious" or "self-evident" usually do not need the additional fanfare. Investigators' self-criticisms can range from empty apologies to insightful commentaries on the merits of the work. Some discussions contain so many modifying adjectives and qualifying phrases, the study swoons with dizzy indecision. "There may seem," "it might hopefully appear," "although evidence may be lacking," and "it may be generally considered to be" head a long list of qualifiers that weaken not only the writing style but the force of the message as well. Another kind of troublesome hedging occurs when, after laboring through the entire paper, we are told that the "results are only preliminary at this time," or that "the numbers studied may be too small to extract meaningful conclusions." Qualifications like these are defended on the grounds that authors are trying not to overstate their case or make unsubstantiated claims. The intent is honest enough. Unfortunately, disclaimers that are tacked on to the final paragraphs of a piece offer readers no constructive alternatives for interpreting results. When authors quaver in their resolve, it shakes our confidence as well. We are left uncertain about the importance of the message. Do they really believe in their work? Is it useful news for clinicians? How could it be improved, or made meaningful?

On the other hand, genuine, constructive, criticism fosters confidence. It is reassuring when authors critically analyze their methods and interpretations. In a study reporting the "decreased risk of fractures of the hip and lower forearm with post-menopausal use of estrogens," Weiss et al. head their discussion with a section entitled, "Limitations of the Data" [9]. They greet potential problems in this study head-on, describing possible biases and shortcomings in their work and assessing the effects of these upon interpretation.

In collecting information from cases and controls about estrogen use, systematic differences occurred. Women who had sustained fractures (cases) were interviewed on average one year after the fracture had occurred. However, they were asked to report estrogen use only until the time they sustained the broken bone. Controls, on the other hand, reported estrogen use until the time of interview. The authors worried that cases might have reported less estrogen usage because of the lapses of memory that occur with time rather than because of real differences in taking the medication. To attack this problem, they reanalyzed their data after removing the potential information bias. They dropped information about control subjects' use of estrogens for the year immediately prior to interview. Lower estrogen use among women with fractures was still demonstrated, supporting the beneficial effects of estrogens.

Another example of the make-it-tough-on-yourself approach can be seen from a further chapter in the saga to improve mortality of patients recovering from heart attack. This time the study is a large collaborative trial conducted in Norway [5]. The drug under scrutiny was timolol, a beta-adrenergic blocking agent. In the trial, over 1,800 patients were randomized to receive either timolol or a placebo beginning in the early recuperative stages following myocardial infarction. Patients were followed for up to 36 months. By the completion of the study, 13.9% of the placebo group experienced sudden death compared to only 7.7% of patients treated with timolol. This was a statistically significant as well as clinically important reduction. However, investigators noted that dropout rates among the two treatment groups were different: more timolol-treated subjects withdrew than placebo-treated subjects. Many of these dropouts were due to adverse side effects of timolol, such as bradycardia and hypotension. The specter of bias raises its unattractive head. Perhaps patients who are sensitive to drug side effects are also susceptible to arrhythmias and sudden death. Dropping them from the analysis when they withdraw from treatment may mean selectively excluding high-risk patients who would have died had they been kept in the study. On the other hand, it is not completely fair to consider them along side their timolol-taking contemporaries since they are, in fact, not under the influence of the drug.

Faced with this dilemma, the investigators did the only sensible thing. They analyzed the data both ways. Mortality rates were compared both for times when patients were actually taking their medication and according to the "intention to treat." Under the intention-to-treat approach, the mortality experience of patients is compared based on their original assignments in the trial without respect to subsequent changes or withdrawal. This is a conservative approach. When results continue to show a beneficial effect for timolol, the argument for success is strengthened.

When we see references to "potential bias in our method" or accounts of "methods for controlling potential confounders," we can tell that authors share some of our critical concerns. Most authors are vested in their research hypothesis. They believe that estrogens reduce fractures and that treating high blood pressure reduces the risk of stroke. It is encouraging when they try alternate methods of analysis and still support their hypothesis.

The Final Word

Regardless of how adamantly authors defend, support, deny, decry, declaim, apologize, or equivocate, we have a perfect right to disagree with their interpretation and offer our own. This disagreement over rights of interpretation need not flow from problems with the paper's methods or analysis. It may simply be a matter of differing opinions over the importance of the findings reported.

The trial of antihistamines for treatment of otitis media reported in chapter 8 is a case in point [6]. Results indicated a statistically significant improvement in resolution of otitis media for patients given the medication, even though only 2 or 3 patients of every 100 were likely to benefit. Another report on the use of antihistamines for the relief of respiratory-tract infections suffers from a similar interpretation dilemma [4]. Investigators in this project developed an elaborate system for treating and observing victims of the common cold. Patients who had "signs and symptoms of the common cold for at least 24 hours" were domiciled in a "supervised environment" for two days so that careful follow-up was possible. Capsules containing either antihistamine or a look-alike placebo were administered to these volunteers, and patients and physicians were queried at various points to see if signs and symptoms had improved. The results, the investigators proclaim, demonstrate that "chlorpheniramine maleate, as a model for antihistamines, is clearly superior to a placebo in providing symptomatic improvement of the common cold." They provide several graphic presentations in support of their claim. Figure 12–1 depicts the physicians' assessment of the symptomatic improvement of cold sufferers. As is characteristic of the other graphs in this presentation, the antihistamine consistently outperforms the placebo. At some points these differences are statistically significant at the chosen alpha level of 0.1 (meaning that the finding could occur by chance 10% of the time). But how important are these differences to clinicians? Do the benefits the authors describe warrant widespread prescribing of antihistamines to patients with self-limited respiratory-tract infections? It is a matter for individual readers to decide. What is one person's "clearly superior" is another person's "may be a little better." It is not a matter of who is right or wrong but of individual opinions.

Consider the interpretation of a study evaluating the benefits of antibiotic treatment of streptococcal sore throat [3]. In this study, patients seen early in the course of streptococcal pharyngitis were randomly allocated to receive penicillin injections, several orally administered tetracyclines, or placebo. The effect of treatment upon signs and symptoms of the disease is displayed in figure 12–2. For the major symptom of sore throat, antibiotic treatment brought consistently quicker relief than placebo. By the fourth day of disease, for example, 65 percent of untreated patients were still complaining of sore throat compared to 25 percent of those given penicillin. Differences in reported symptom rates were statistically unlikely to be due to chance ($p < .01$) for each day after the first day of disease.

Yet, in discussions of the nagging dilemma of when to initiate treatment for strep throat—whether to begin penicillin straight away or wait for results of the throat culture—this study has been used to support the view that prompt therapy produces little in the way of symptomatic relief. In a review of the perplexities of streptococcal pharyngitis, [7] a coauthor of the first study advocates waiting for culture results before treating, since "treatment does not appreciably alter the clinical course of the acute infection." Again the matter is open for debate. Antibiotic-treated strep throats certainly do not all dramatically disappear within 12 to 24 hours, but some clinicians may feel that the clinical course has been altered when 95 percent

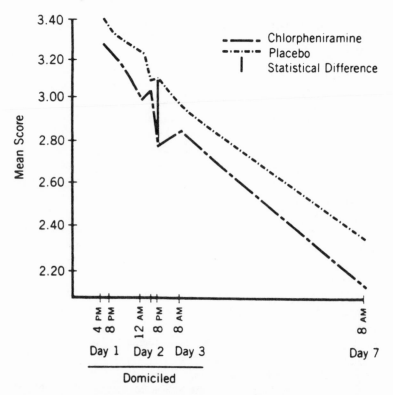

Figure 12–1. *Physicians' global evaluation of patient's condition: 1—excellent (75% to 100% remission of signs and symptoms); 2—good (50% to 75% remission); 3—fair (25% to 50% remission); 4—poor (0% to 25% remission); 5—exacerbation. (From Howard, J. C. et al. [4] JAMA 242:2414–2417, 1979. Copyright © 1979 American Medical Association.)*

of untreated patients are complaining of pharyngitis on the second day of disease compared with 70 percent of those given penicillin. It is a clinical interpretation.

Summary

We are back where we began—with a desktop full of journals, a desire to be knowledgeable, and a distressingly tiny aliquot of time. We have learned some analytic techniques and mastered our fears of inadequacy when confronting the experts. The

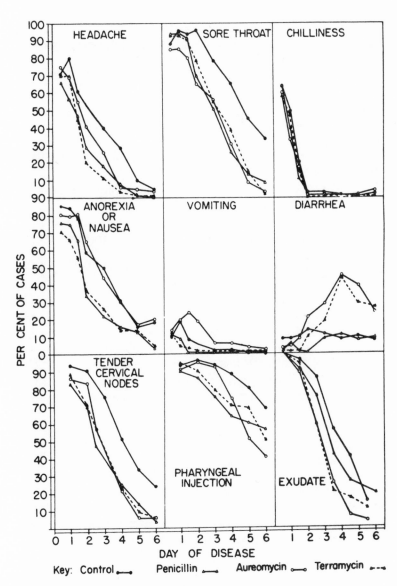

Figure 12-2. *Effect of various antibiotics on symptoms and signs of acute streptococcal tonsillitis and pharyngitis. (From Denny, F. W. et al.* [3] *Pediatrics 11:7–14, 1953. Copyright © 1953 American Academy of Pediatrics.)*

task is formidable, but not impossible. With a little planning, perseverance, and practice, the medical literature can become not only palatable, but downright digestible.

References

1. ARMSTRONG, J. S. Unintelligible management research and academic prestige. *Interfaces* 10:80–86, 1980.

2. CRICHTON, M. Medical obfuscation: Structure and function. *N. Engl. J. Med.* 293:1257–1259, 1975.

3. DENNY, F. W., WANNAMAKER, L. W., AND HAHN, E. O. Comparative effects of penicillin, Aureomycin and Terramycin on streptococcal tonsillitis and pharyngitis. *Pediatrics* 11:7–14, 1953.

4. HOWARD, J. C., KANTNER, T. R., LILIENFIELD, L. S., ET AL. Effectiveness of antihistamines in the symptomatic management of the common cold. *JAMA* 242:2414–2417, 1979.

5. NORWEGIAN MULTICENTER STUDY GROUP. Timolol-induced reduction in mortality and reinfarction in patients surviving acute myocardial infarction. *N. Engl. J. Med.* 304:801–807, 1981.

6. STICKLER, G. B., RUBENSTEIN, M. M., MCBEAN, J. B., HEDGECOCK, L. D., HUGSTAD, J. A., AND GRIFFIN, T. Treatment of acute otitis media in children. IV. A fourth clinical trial. *Amer. J. Dis. Child.* 114:123–130, 1967.

7. WANNAMAKER, L. W. Perplexity and precision in the diagnosis of streptococcal pharyngitis. *Amer. J. Dis. Child.* 124:352–358, 1972.

8. WARE, J. E. AND WILLIAMS, R. G. The Dr. Fox effect: A study of lecturer effectiveness and ratings of instruction. *J. Med. Educ.* 50:149–156, 1975.

9. WEISS, N. S., URE, C. L., BALLARD, J. H., WILLIAMS, A. R., AND DALING, J. R. Decreased risk of fractures of the hip and lower forearm with postmenopausal use of estrogen. *N. Engl. J. Med.* 303:1195–1198, 1980.

Index

Index